Praise for *The Lengthening War*

In the preface to the second volume of his World War Two diary, James Lees-Milne, arguably the greatest British diarist of his time, laid down the ground rules for diary-keeping. 'A diary', he wrote, '… is necessarily spasmodic and prosaic. But it must be spontaneous. It must not be doctored … it will be full of inconsistencies and contradictions. It reflects the author's shifting moods, tastes, prejudices and even beliefs, too few of which he remains constant for long.' The First World War diary of Mabel Goode meets all these criteria and more. It offers a superb contemporary portrait of a nation coming to terms with the demands of total war. To the historian it offers fresh evidence of how life was lived on the home front during the First World War, complete with the most extraordinary rumours and misplaced optimism. Thus on the 12th September 1914, we read that '… one really does not see how the War can go on much longer. The French say it will be over Christmas. It seems quite likely.' The diary also offers readers not only the minutiae of Britain at war including the rise in food and fuel prices, but vivid accounts of the Zeppelin raids. Personally, one has only two regrets. The first, that the diary stops in December 1916, with news of the fall of Romania to the Central Powers and the accession of Lloyd George, ('I don't trust LG but he has great energy& will probably get things done …'), to the premiership. The second, that Mabel's diary was not available to me when I was writing my history of the British home front, 1914–1918. Extracts from it would have undoubtedly enhanced my own account. But at least it is now available to the historian and to the general reader alike, both of whom will delight in it. And I have no doubt that it will have an honourable place on the history shelves alongside the diaries of Ethel Bilbrough and Georgina Lee and the works of Constance Peel and Caroline Playne in giving us such a splendidly readable picture of Britain at war a century ago.

Terry Charman, former Senior Historian at the Imperial War Museum and author of The First World War on the Home Front 1914–18

The Lengthening War

This book is dedicated to my Grandparents and my Mother who made me the man I am today.

The book also comes with special thanks to the following for their patience, insight and friendship:

*James M. Wakeley who is the Sam to my Frodo, the Frodo to my Sam, and a **profoundly** good friend all round*

Hetty Saunders whose wit and fortitude bring a beauty more powerful than any source of despair

Professor Andrew Blake who means more to me than he will ever know

Professor Menderes Çinar & Reyhan Ünal who are beginning to mean more to me than they will ever know

Dr Sian Pooley for her careful advice and endurance

Louise Jones who is the best lexical guinea pig a chap could ask for

Anni Ludhra whose eagle eye and positivity are to be treasured for the wonders they are

Jake Richards who is both one of the smartest and one of the most decent people I know

Jack Wiseman, Tara Smith, Jordan Sisson and Joey Chavoshi-Nasab for being with me in the library (along with Marc Hobbs and Ryan Baker for being there in spirit)

The author would also like to thank both Tony Allen & the Brighton and Hove Collection for their kind generosity in allowing the reproduction of their images

And finally, I'd like to mention my sister Jasmine, who I'm sure will grow up to be every bit as creative and talented as Mabel

The Lengthening War

The Great War Diary of Mabel Goode

By Michael Goode

Foreword by Sir Chris Clark, Regius Professor of
History, Cambridge University

PEN & SWORD
HISTORY

First published in Great Britain in 2016 by
Pen & Sword History
an imprint of
Pen & Sword Books Ltd
47 Church Street
Barnsley
South Yorkshire
S70 2AS

Copyright © Michael Goode 2016

ISBN 978 1 47385 151 1

A CIP catalogue record for this book is available from the British
Library

Typeset in Ehrhardt by
Mac Style Ltd, Bridlington, East Yorkshire
Printed and bound in the UK by CPI Group (UK) Ltd,
Croydon, CRO 4YY

Pen & Sword Books Ltd incorporates the imprints of Pen & Sword
Archaeology, Atlas, Aviation, Battleground, Discovery, Family
History, History, Maritime, Military, Naval, Politics, Railways, Select,
Transport, True Crime, and Fiction, Frontline Books, Leo Cooper,
Praetorian Press, Seaforth Publishing and Wharncliffe.

For a complete list of Pen & Sword titles please contact
PEN & SWORD BOOKS LIMITED
47 Church Street, Barnsley, South Yorkshire, S70 2AS, England
E-mail: enquiries@pen-and-sword.co.uk
Website: www.pen-and-sword.co.uk

Contents

August 11th 1914 Tuesday.

What a time! Never has there been anything so tremendous in the History of Europe before. And it has all come about within the last 10 days, certainly as far as England is concerned.

A week ago last Saturday, Henry & I were enjoying ourselves at the Archbishops Garden Party at Bishopthorpe & there was only a sufficient darkening of the horizon with war clouds to form a main topic of conversation & make things interesting.

Now, 10 days later War has been declared between England, France & Russia & Germany, the long-expected War, come suddenly, as long-expected things generally do & 2,000,000 soldiers are facing each other with grim determination for 300 miles along the dividing frontier of France & Germany.

York is full of soldiers, all the larger spaces & buildings are being used as barracks

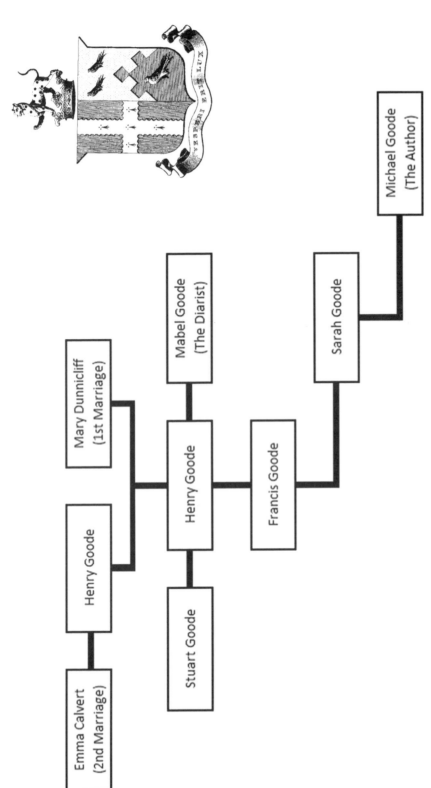

Figures 2 & 3: Family diagram showing the author's connection to the diarist and the family shield.

'Zeus, whose will has marked for man
 The sole way where wisdom lies;
 Ordered one eternal plan:
 Man must suffer to be wise.'
                    – Aeschylus, *Agamemnon*, 458 BC

Foreword

'The great battle has not yet begun, but all the news so far is good', Mabel Goode wrote in her diary on 17 August. 'The Germans & Austrians are being drawn back on all sides ...' Mabel was impressed by the 'million bags of flour' sent by the Canadians and the emergency hospitals springing up all over the country, but she couldn't help wondering whether all the fuss was really necessary: 'One wonders a little, will it really be all wanted?' One week later, reports that the French and British had fallen back in Belgium dispelled her insouciance. 'The first important news is bad,' she wrote. 'It is sad, as it will certainly prolong the war'.

The war that raged without cease for the next four years was the primal catastrophe of the twentieth century. It destroyed four world empires, consumed the lives of at least ten million young men and wounded between fifteen and twenty-one million more. Without it, it is hard to imagine the ascent of Fascism to power in Italy, or the October Revolution in Russia and the subsequent establishment of a one-party Bolshevik state with no precedent in world history. Without the deep ruptures of war, defeat and revolution, German history would surely not have followed its catastrophic course into dictatorship, war and mass extermination.

The fascination of this diary lies in the fact that it enables us to trace the history of Britain's home front through the eyes of a lucid contemporary. Mabel Goode was a middle-class woman living with her mother and her brother, Henry, who was a doctor in York. She was interested in the great events of her time: the sinking of the Lusitania, the defeat of Romania by the Germans, the war in Russia and the Balkans. Some of this was gleaned from the newspapers, but much of her news came from conversations with friends and acquaintances. She interweaves her thoughts on these great matters with poignant observations of life at home in wartime: the food shortages, the Zeppelin raids, the anxious pursuit of the latest news, not just of events, but of loved ones, friends and acquaintances fighting at the front. The war did not suspend ordinary life entirely, but it is astonishing to see how completely it dominated the awareness of contemporaries, squeezing out everything else. Sympathy with men at the front, fear for their welfare and joy in their victories, pity for those who had already lost loved ones, rage at the enemy, whose atrocities were the subject of detailed press reports, the pervasive fear of air attack and an oppressive sense of the fragility of life suffuse this chronicle, as we register the deepening weariness of a woman for whom war gradually becomes an all-embracing existential condition. In December 1914, a friend lent her the score of a waltz to play on the piano, but she had little confidence that the opportunity would arise to play it. 'People are not thinking of valses this winter & there will, I suppose, be very few balls'.

Chris Clark, Cambridge 2015

Selected List of People Featured in the Diary

Family:
Mabel (Diarist, see 'About the Diarist' section), *Henry* (elder brother, see 'Henry' section), *Mother* (see 'About the Diarist' section), *Stuart* (eldest brother, see 'Stuart' section), *'Rags'* (the dog)

Servants:
Price (housemaid), *Nancy* (housemaid), *Evans* (with family from 1893, servant, retired in 1915), *Imeson* (with family from 1904, carriage-driver and chauffeur for Henry's Daimler car, later joins the Army Service Corps as Motor Ambulance Driver, then returns temporarily, left in 1919), *Kathleen* (maid)

Local:
Mr Shann (also known as Dr Shann, father of Rosetta who became Henry's wife), *Captain Lister* (a chaplain, friend of Henry's and likely to be the chaplain featured on the front cover), *Mr Campbell* (a neighbour and later a chaplain for the 2nd West Riding Brigade)

Friends of Mabel:
Miss Barry, Mrs Dunnington-Jefferson, Colonel and Mrs Jencken, the Haywards (lived near Swanage); *Delia Place* (and *May Place*, Lady Superintendent)

Friends and colleagues of Henry:
Captain Stewart (later Major Stewart, 'Stewey'), *Major Sharpe* (later Colonel Sharpe), *Lieutenant Pope, Lieutenant Hughes* ('Hughey', set up a field hospital with Henry in 1915)

Introduction:
A Short Diary of a Lengthening War

'The lamps are going out all over Europe, we shall not see them lit again
in our life-time'

Attributed to Sir Edward Grey, British Foreign Secretary

In 1913 the lamps of Europe burned with a bright light, a light of
intellectualism, a light of culture, a light of progress. This cluster of nations
and empires in the north west of Eurasia dominated the world in a way
not seen before or since: in 1913 Europe accounted for forty-seven per cent
of the world's GDP and twenty-nine per cent of its population,[1] and the
people of Europe had been getting richer, healthier and better educated in
record numbers since 1870. My first introduction to these lamps, and their
snuffing out, came from a passing conversation several years ago, which has
stayed with me ever since. I used to have history-related discussions with a
Professor close to our family. One day, I was going through a tower of his
books; one caught my eye: *Nineteenth-Century European Civilization, 1815–
1914* by Geoffrey Bruun. Excited, I omitted the first section of the title and
read aloud: 'European Civilisation, 1815–1914'. My friend half laughed and
said: 'Because that's when it ended.' It does not take much understanding
of the First World War to see just how much truth was in that sentiment. It
may not even be too much to say that *a* civilisation, although certainly not
civilisation itself, did indeed die in that conflict.[2]

What remains of that civilisation are the artefacts it produced and the
memories they contain. It is hard to describe what it is first like to handle
a personal diary from another era. Going through its pages, their entries
handwritten on dates approximately (and in some cases exactly) one
hundred years ago, the words and the scenes described seemed eerily alive.
Yet in reading the diary it is clear that, due to the very war it describes,

its world has passed. Despite the immense efforts of the centenary events surrounding 2014–18, we struggle to understand some of the paradoxes of that momentous conflict and grasp the flavour of such a distant age. It was with that thought in mind that what started out in 2011 as a project to honour my great-great-Aunt Mabel, by typing up her diary for my family to read, became something much broader.

Reading a diary can pull you into another's existence; however inscrutable someone's life appeared previously, you are now reading their thoughts, hearing about their day and, before long, finding yourself immersed in their own personal mix of aspirations, worries and observations. This diary has several themes, which make its account revealing far beyond the purely personal sphere. It gives us insight into how the Great War was portrayed and experienced directly, as it happened, day by day.

Mabel's writings (as a single middle-class woman in her early forties, living with her mother and brother in York) show us just how vast the gulf was between the trenches and the Home Front. Despite having lived in Germany from 1881 to 1887, she fully accepted and recorded the newspaper accounts of German atrocities and barbarism, indicating what the British heard about and thought of their main enemy. Moreover, even with a brother at the Front, Mabel frequently believed the war effort was going much better than we now know to be true. What Mabel saw and understood of the conflict shows us what partial truths filtered back to the Home Front and what stories emerged from the fog of war. Her perspective helps us to understand the frustration some soldiers felt at how incomprehensible the Front was to those at home.

To Mabel, the war was not just some distant event reported in the newspapers: her diary records the ways in which her life changed due to the pressures imposed on her by the conflict. One by one, the family saw their domestic servants leave; yet the same pressures that took Mabel's servants also led her to new and novel experiences. Tellingly, as an older middle-class woman, Mabel undertook taxing manual labour for the first time in her life, due to the lack of men on the Home Front. The war undermined some previous certainties and piled on new obligations, as some social and occupational roles vanished and others were remade.

The work Mabel did for the war effort and the ways her life changed were given new meaning when the enemy came to her. Mabel wrote of the fear brought by conflict which, for the first time, meant not just a dreaded telegram from the Front but also the enemy's weapons of war (a Zeppelin above a city, or a battleship off the coast) which threatened civilian life and communities. The diary takes us through the emotions of those first aerial attacks, sharing what it was like for a civilian born in the late Victorian era to see, in the first war of its kind, a huge enemy machine hovering overhead, threatening death. The profound psychological impact of this threat – combined with everyday challenges such as the rising food prices of a strained economy and the mobilisation of the nation for the war effort – conveys the totality of this war.

The above highlights three themes which give the reader a good insight into what it was like to experience the First World War from a woman's perspective: what she saw of and knew about the conflict; what it took from her and what she did for it; and how the war came all too close to her. Entry by entry we see how the conflict progressed, the life that continued parallel to it and the toll that it took.

The diary's real beauty is just that: it is a diary, a record of one person's experiences over time. Above all else, its importance lies in taking us through the progression of the war, in telling us what the war meant to Britain when Mabel began writing in the summer of 1914 and how it was transformed through the years as the war unleashed unprecedented destruction, despair and death. The crucial word in the last sentence is 'unprecedented', because for most in 1914 it translated into 'totally unexpected'. In this war, another shade is added to the spectrum of tragedy when it is understood what preceded it. The eminent historian Lord Blake captured this in saying:

Mankind has all down history looked back nostalgically to the golden ages of the past. Under the scrutiny of the historian these tend to dissolve into mere dreams, but there is one which deserves some claim to reality: the forty-three years of peace, progress and prosperity between 1871 and 1914 were, for most of Europe anyway, a genuine golden age.[3]

We keep turning back to the First World War because of the world and the lives it shattered, because of the vast amount of unforeseen death it caused:

total figures suggest at least ten million military deaths and a further fifteen to twenty-one million combatants wounded.[4] Historians are still trying to work out where to place the blame, or how well generals led their men, because we feel a need to justify these immense losses and allocate guilt for them. These debates are so deeply contested and protracted because no individual, group or nation wants such blood on their hands and there seems no natural home for such blame. Nothing captures this better than the debate over whether Germany started the war.[5]

Yet, as with other (but not all) historical events, the war lives on because it also commands attention far beyond academic circles. There are many across Europe for whom the First World War still commands much thought in their heads and much sorrow in their hearts. It is an absurdity to think that the First World War completely ended on 11 November 1918: millions of personal battles with what that conflict created, or took away, continued past the Armistice and some even continue to this day. In terms of unexpected deaths alone, stirring images (real or imagined) of thousands upon thousands of men eagerly (and occasionally prematurely) signing up – striving to do their bit or have a dash for glory, unable to envisage the stagnant spells of watching, waiting and dying on the Western Front – provide one of the reasons for the bitterness and sorrow which still surrounds the war. When a civilisation loses millions of its own, questions must be answered. Despite this, our collective memory of the war is distorted by our proclivity to focus on the major events linked to these deaths. David Reynolds states that for Britain imagining the war typically means picturing the first day of the Somme.[6] The retrospective attempt to make sense of the war is understandable, but it skews our understanding of what it was like to live through that struggle, to know it as a dynamic unfolding rather than a few titanic events.

This book does not seek to address the above issues directly but rather to tell a story through the diary. Mabel's first-hand account captures just how unforeseen the nature of this war was. The greatest strength of the diary lies in Mabel's gradual realisation that the war was inescapably lengthening and mutating into unprecedented horror. After the First Battle of the Marne (5–12 September 1914), ideals of a short struggle were blown apart on the fields of France and Belgium. As the war became stationary, it found itself in unplanned territory. While to us, attrition and stagnation are synonymous with the Western Theatre, Mabel and the rest of the population did not know what was around the corner. What Mabel gives us is an understanding of the real fascination and excitement with the war in its early days, along with the steady realisation that vast gains were not being made, men were dying and costs were mounting.

Mabel stopped writing her diary in 1916. We cannot know for certain her reason for abandoning it when she did. Yet it is unlikely to be a mere coincidence that the diary stops when a quick end was no longer in sight (shortly after the failure of the large scale Allied offensive known as the Great Push, a low-point in the war of attrition) and in the year that the War Office commandeered the family home for its use. What we do know is that what had started with a flurry of eager writing became more and more despairing, increasingly infrequent and eventually ceased altogether. From this we gain more insight into the real experiences had by Mabel and others, rather than the one-dimensional historical snapshots (weighted with searching questions) comparing the giddy spirit of 1914 with a weary 1918.

Figure 4: Early postcard from 1914 showing the sentiments expressed at the start of the war. (*Tony Allen's Postcard Collection*)

Chapter 1

The Disappearance of the Spirit of 1914

'It takes 15,000 casualties to train a major general.'
Attributed to Marshal Ferdinand Foch

In order to understand the metamorphosis the war underwent and how different its growth was to expectations, we must look at the diary's opening and the spirit with which the country went to war. There is considerable debate about the spirit in which the British people responded to the outbreak of war and its early days. What emerges from the opening passages of the diary, however, is remarkably strong and consistent. Mabel is engaged with, and enthused by, the reports coming from the continent. She eagerly embraces news of the nation readying itself for war. It would not be impossible to say that the whole thing enthrals her.

The excitement of the start

Mabel might not have known what lay ahead in 1914 but she certainly realised the war's significance as the most important event to happen in her lifetime. This is immediately apparent in the diary's opening lines: 'Never has there been anything so tremendous in the History of Europe'.[1] Referring to the war as 'long expected' in her first entry on 11 August hints at just how pregnant the summer of 1914 was with the struggle. The care and attention Mabel gives to the outbreak of war and the beginning of her diary to record its events is indicative of the seriousness with which she and others took the news. The rapid unfurling of the two fighting blocs and the hasty mobilisation of troops – the sheer swiftness of the start of the war – is captured in the pace of Mabel's early entries. We see the growing momentum of events, as Mabel notes on 18 August that the news was developing faster than the newspapers could keep up with: 'Several editions of the 'Press' have been published every day at short intervals ever since the war began'. To Mabel, the war merited putting pen to paper because it was both apprehensively awaited and utterly thrilling as it developed day by day.

A short war?

Mabel clearly thought the war would not last long. On 30 August 1914 – twenty-nine days after the war started – she wrote that the news sounded like the 'beginning of the end'. Initially, Mabel held onto this belief. On 12 September she wrote 'one really does not see how the War can go on very much longer. The French say it will be over by Christmas. It seems quite likely'. Not alone in this, she noted earlier, on 8 September, that Major Sharpe (one of her brother's senior officers) 'thinks the war will last 6 months'. Not all of the voices were so optimistic; her brother Henry felt the war would last a year, but Mabel dismissed this, having written on 12 September that 'the wish is father to the thought.... he is anxious for the war to last, or rather, to get out [to France] before the war ends'. It is only as the war went on that Mabel started to question the prospect of a short conflict. The first sense of this came on 1 November: 'The War has been going on for nearly 3 months now, & it seems likely to be longer than ever'. Passage after passage reveals how Mabel increasingly doubted that the war would be over by Christmas: a process that shows the gradual death of the excitement and optimism that characterised the Spirit of 1914. In an entry on 30 November, Mabel records that Henry and a servant are tucking up the car 'for its long rest' and then, giving a sense of growing doubt and caution, she decided to add 'How long? I wonder'.

Why Britain went to war and who she was fighting

As the illusion of a short war was shattered, so was Mabel's perception of the Germans. In the Spirit of 1914, Mabel draws strength from a feeling that the war was righteous; writing on 18 August that 'It is a great thing to feel that our cause is a just one & one may genuinely believe that God has helped us, for things are wonderfully in our favour. ... It is the cause of progress, peace & civilisation against militarism & despotism'. Viewing why we went to war in these terms helps contextualise the patriotism expressed on the outbreak of the conflict. To Mabel, it seemed that the war was distant and unthreatening and that the enemy could be managed and defeated. On the suggestion of an invasion threat, Mabel wrote on 21 August 1914 that, given the forces on the Western and Eastern Fronts, 'one can only think they [the Germans] will have all they can do not to be completely crushed'. Again, her tune starts to change by 7 May 1915; after writing about German artillery, Mabel admits that 'They are a more formidable foe than I expected', a sentiment which must have been shared by many.

Escalation from stagnation

The tragedy of a large-scale and ground-breaking conflict like the First World War is that it becomes like a ratchet that can only be turned one way: it locks itself into intensification as more and more die in its battles, making negotiation and peace less and less likely, because leaders must convey that those deaths were not in vain. Thus, ever-increasing resources and people are spent on an all-out victory to justify the cost which, when done by both sides, leads to nothing but further spiralling. If half measures were ever an option, they could not survive in such a climate. That was the nature of this war.

Mabel had a real sense of the role technology would play in changing the parameters of this war. She wrote on 25 October 1914 that 'The great battle on the Belgian coast is still in progress, the first in history in which there has been fighting on land, on sea & in the air all at the same time'. She had known smaller-scale colonial conflicts through one brother (Stuart) being a professional soldier and the other (Henry) serving as a surgeon in the Boer War. However, the extent to which new technology would allow this war to dwarf the scale of what had been before was yet to be seen.

The evolving nature of the war, transformed through industry and technology, led Mabel to write of new and ghastly evils (seemingly a world away from the noble sentiments illustrated in figure 4). She mentions the growth of industrial chemical warfare as early as 7 May 1915 with the comments:

The effects of the asphyxiating gas used by the Germans near Ypres is too horrible. Those who do not die at once, suffer from slow, increasing suffocation, lasting sometimes one or 2 days … It is the most horrible form of scientific torture. And those who do not die from the suffocation, always suffer from acute pneumonia. What fiends they are! They say half the soldiers who came into hospital suffering from gas only, quite unwounded, have died.

When the war came to civilians, Mabel condemned the German behaviour and, on 16 May, recorded how this changed the public feeling about the war, saying:

> This cold-blooded murder of civilians at sea & the use of the poisonous gases have quite altered the feeling of our troops towards the Germans. Before there was a good-natured dislike & tolerance, but now there is a bitter hatred & a demand for reprisals.

WHICH IS THE QUICKEST WAY TO THE HOSPITAL MY BOY ?

STAND IN THE ROAD AND SHOUT "THREE CHEERS FOR THE KAISER". SIR.

Figure 5: Making light of the growing anti-German sentiments in wartime Britain. (*Tony Allen's WWI Postcard Collection*)

Indeed, the horrors of the escalating war, and an increasingly desperate Germany, did lead to reprisals and spontaneous public anger (made light of in figure 5). Mabel went on to mention in the same entry that 'Since Lusitania was sunk there have been many anti-German riots & shops wrecked & large numbers of the enemy aliens have been interned'.

The mounting casualty lists

As the war changed, so did the public's perception of it. Essential to this process was the fact that as the war enveloped more men, it became personally significant to more and more families up and down the country who now had a relative fighting. The diary gradually traces this growing realisation that the war will be a longer, harder and altogether more desperate affair than expected. The turning point seems to come alongside a tangibly more intense anxiety for Mabel's brother's welfare. On 16 May 1915 she wrote: 'it is indeed a terrible war & it will be almost a miracle if he [Henry] comes back unscathed'.

Typical for families across the nation, this fear of loss added a personal concern to the frustrating lack of progress Mabel mentions time and time again. On 27 June 1915, Mabel sums up her feeling that the war was both costly and futile: 'One must admit that we have not got very far yet in moving the Germans either East or West', adding: 'Our losses each day are terrible, both officers & men. Generally between 100 & 200 officers every day in the Casualty List, & yet so little to show for it!' This feeling lingered, as she adds nearly a month later on 26 July that 'the West side is practically in status quo'. In marked contrast to the excitement of the first few entries of 1914, these unhappy observations give way to critical comments, almost certainly aided by the fact that Mabel's brother was now in uniform. On 1 August 1915, Mabel wrote: 'We seem quite unable to do more than hold them. I suppose on account of want of guns & shells. It has been a most disappointing year on the West, to my mind'.

Mabel's thoughts were, however, not entirely negative. She added ten days after this entry that it was the Allies, not the Central Powers, who could ultimately sustain a longer war. What would prove to be her, largely vindicated, thoughts on the balance of resources encouraged her to believe that the Germans' 'turn will come'. Nonetheless, the incompetent handling of the battles around Salonica (which failed to prevent the fall of Serbia), provoked Mabel to write on 28 November 1915 that 'We always seem to leave things to fate & suddenly wake up when the harm is done, instead of preventing it. Another terrible waste of valuable lives & time.'

Disengagement

Even as the war's longevity surpassed expectations, all Mabel could do on hearing the latest news was to conclude that it would last longer still. On 25 August 1914, Mabel wrote that the Allies had failed to decisively deal with the enemy: 'So the first important news is bad just when we had hoped that the Allies would have inflicted a crushing defeat on the Germans. It is sad, as it will certainly prolong the war'. On 1 November 1914 she recorded Turkey's coming in against the Allies and the Boer rebellion, stating 'Of course all these things will lengthen the war'. By 6 June 1915 the shell shortage worried Mabel a great deal, as she recorded 'I fear it will very much prolong the war & cause terrible loss of valuable lives, all alas! our best'. A little later, on 27 June 1915, the bad news from the Eastern Front again pushes victory further away from Mabel, who wrote: 'The Germans & Austrians under General von Mackensen have retaken Lemberg, which was taken by the Russians as long ago as September 2nd. Of course they are rejoicing greatly. It will certainly lengthen the war & cheer our enemies, which is very unfortunate'. This is reinforced on 1 August 1915 when the losses on the Eastern Front cause Mabel to write again: 'It is a great triumph for the enemy & will doubtless lengthen the War very much' and on the 11 August 'Of course it will lengthen the war'.

The unfolding events Mabel recorded progressively blotted out her hopes of a swift victory. The spectre of sustained Allied defeats was so alien to the expectations of the general British public at the start of the war that the optimism, which characterised the Spirit of 1914, was forced to eventually give up the ghost. To a woman who had been born into the certainty and self-confidence of Victorian Britain at its imperial apogee, the lengthening war must have stretched ever forward into a new and more frightening world.

As Mabel saw the war lengthen, so she saw it change. She saw it emerge as a struggle worse than anything she and her peers had imagined. She saw the costs mounting and the failure to make gains in spite of tremendous effort and sacrifice. As with so many others, the spirit of enthusiasm and excitement, evident in the diary's early passages, faded. What replaced them, in Mabel's case, was a mixture of confusion at the handling of the war, bitterness towards an enemy that seemed to turn its back on the rules of the game, and criticism of a lack of Allied progress. All of these things fed into one growing theme: apathy. Just as the above entries demonstrate Mabel's change of tone, as the Spirit of 1914 is eroded, so the chart in figure 6 shows that, as the war went on, she paid less attention to her diary. Each year the gap between entries steadily increases, and those terser, gloomier entries of 1915 and 1916 look increasingly different from the sort of language used in 1914.

While the diary gives us much more than a personal insight into that sapping of the Spirit of 1914, it is the despondency evident in its pages which is the major message we can take from Mabel. As time, blood and funds are spent,

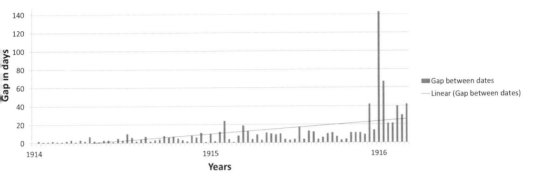

Figure 6: Gap between entry dates. (The spike in early 1916 is linked to the death of Mabel's mother.)

the view from Mabel's Home Front turns away from whole-hearted patriotism, firstly to a questioning of management, then to a loss of interest and finally to a general disengagement. Entries were written further and further apart and with less enthusiasm until, eventually, they stopped altogether.

Comments from the final few entries set the tone, as Mabel observed on 29 October 1916 that 'It is too wet & muddy now for the Allies to make much progress in the West, though they continue to move forward. Henry says they think the War may last another 2 years' and from the final passage: 'With Roumania in German hands, the war may go on another 3 years, apparently'. Mabel sums up the whole picture in the silence of the empty pages where the 1917 and 1918 entries should be. That silence is the furthest she got, and could get, from those long, detailed and upbeat opening entries.

Mabel's final entry in 1916 also gives us a fascinating insight into something we now find very hard to understand: what it was like to live through the First World War not knowing whether you would win, but instead knowing that things were going much worse than expected. In itself, Mabel's diary is a record of disengagement, as the war becomes something altogether new, unprecedented in scale and horror and, for Mabel at the time of writing, seemingly with no end in sight. Yet even though the diary came to a premature end, it is still with us today. The diary outlived Mabel, much as the war itself outlived the diarist's willingness to record it, and much as the memory of the war continues to outlive the many who were lost in those traumatic four years.

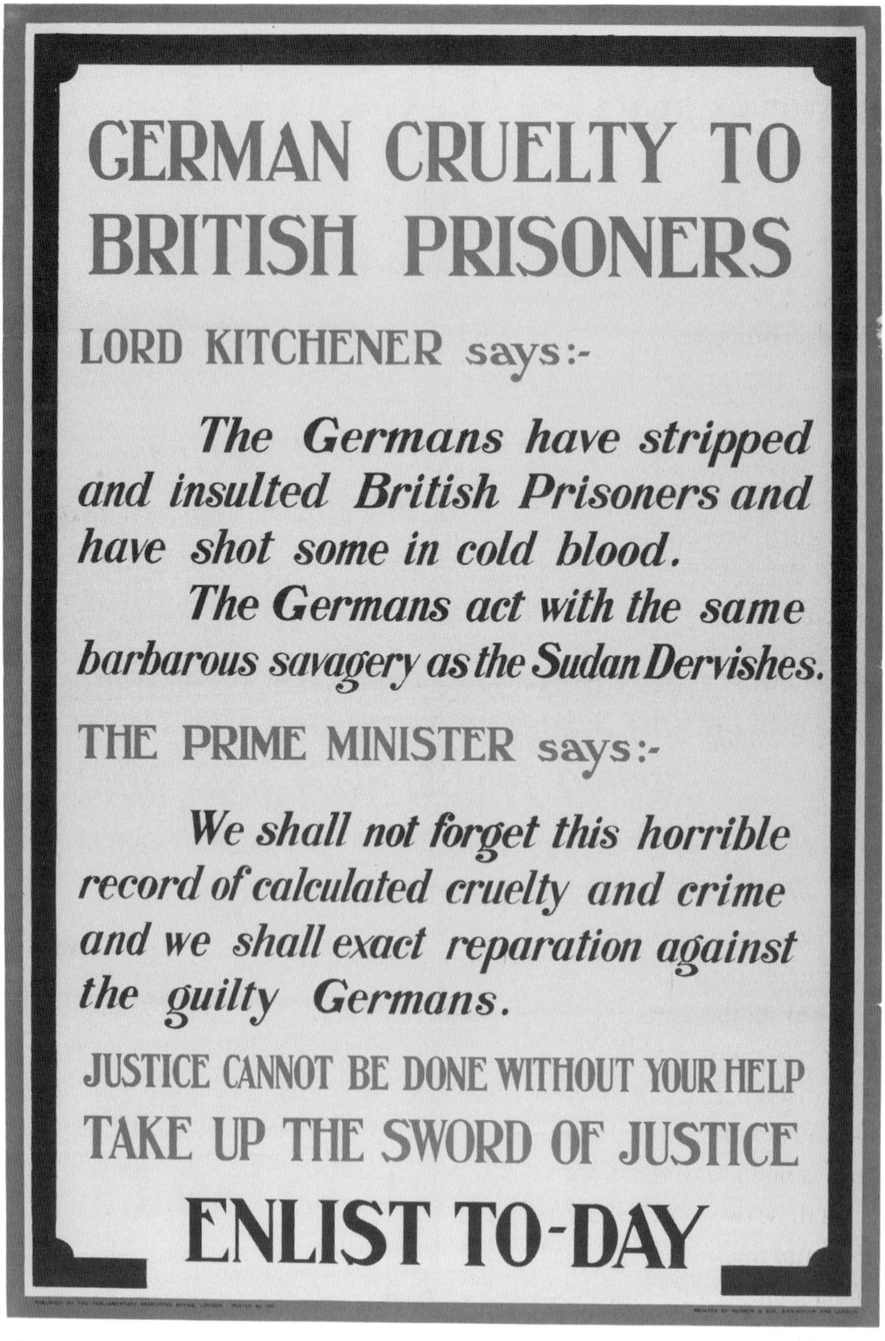

Figure 7: Recruitment poster from 1915, highlighting the reported injustices of the Germans. (*Royal Pavilion & Museums Brighton & Hove*)

Chapter 2

Worlds Apart: Mabel's View and the Reality

'News is what somebody somewhere wants to suppress; all the rest is advertising.'

Lord Northcliffe (1865–1922), Newspaper Magnate

Two different wars

The war recorded in the pages of Mabel's diary was not the war that took place. War means different things to different people, largely because of the information they have to hand, which is why in times of war, propaganda and news control become so important. Even after her brothers began service, the diary shows that Mabel predominately used official channels and home networks for her war news. We now know of the disparity between official news and reality. *The Times's* report on the first day of the Battle of the Somme exemplifies this. Britain had suffered around 60,000 casualties but the coverage was buoyant: 'Everything has gone well ... Our troops have successfully carried out their missions, all counter-attacks have been repulsed and large numbers of prisoners taken'.[1] Mabel herself echoes these sentiments by writing six days later 'The fighting is not quite so severe now as it was on the 1st & 2nd of July, as our men & the French are consolidating their positions, which the Germans have lost & been unable to regain'. The discrepancies between what Mabel read and what we know to be true indicates both the level of misinformation present and how hard it was then (and is now) to understand the war, because effectively two wars existed.

Of these two wars, it is the one on the Home Front that is the harder to recreate or comprehend, because it is an imagined (and to some extent constructed) understanding stretched over a wider variety of people and experiences. Simply put, most Britons read about Germans rather than shot at them. Yet the diary can only go so far in recreating this mentality as, unlike civilian contemporaries, we struggle to understand what it was like to live through the conflict.

Information travels in streams: facts, insights and observations are connected to other pieces of knowledge and the flow reveals itself over time. While both torrents are tampered with, hindsight offers a flood of information, as opposed to the contemporary having a mere trickle. We have all the surviving knowledge available, we are not waiting for events to unfold and, most importantly, we know the conclusion. As a result of this privileged knowledge, we can lose a sense of the seriousness of the time. Think of the uncertainty of a close election or big football match and then how quickly that special sense of unknowing evaporates – and how hard it is to recapture – once the outcome is clear. The closest most people in the post-war generations have come to this destabilising sense of uncertainty may be the distress of personal circumstances, such as waiting for the result of a diagnosis or a looming tragedy. It is hard to capture the sense of a whole country – and indeed a whole continent – living day by day with the hope and despair of war over long years. We lose what it was like to actually live through every ominous day of the war, not knowing the outcome. Mabel had no such luxury. From the very start of the diary, she weighed up evidence from newspapers, personal rumours, and letters from the Front, in order to capture the prevailing thoughts and to try to make sense of events.

Although Mabel relied on the news, in 1914 it was far from a static and measured source. Mabel highlighted this two weeks after the outbreak of war, having written that she bought two or three different editions of newspapers a day: 'they only cost ½ d. Today the 'Evening Press' was being sold in the streets at 12a.m.!' It is comments like these that provide a real sense of what it was like to be alive in mid-August 1914. The momentum of events was gathering at such a rate that newspapers were published several times a day. Editors felt there was enough fresh news to report that they went to print again within a few hours after the last paper. We live in the age of twenty-four hour news; stories break and unravel in front of our eyes and reporters have been criticised for second-guessing a story rather than waiting to be in possession of the facts. The summer of 1914 was a world away from this. To get this close to a rolling news situation in the press shows how the development of events forced the papers to change the way they did business and suggests just how little of what was reported could have been irrefutably true. Just as with our media now, when the news is moving at such speed and what is reported is so political, truth and accuracy suffer. From this reporting, a new and different war was created in the minds of most Britons.

The Germans

Ideas of German barbarity were extremely important in galvanising support for the war, mobilising populations and convincing people they were on the right side. German atrocities would have been one of the answers Mabel gave to the question 'why did we fight?' and it was an answer certainly used to cement support for the war. (As displayed in figures 7 and 9.) Germany's sneering at international law was another (as illustrated by figure 29). Mabel saw the conflict in very black and white terms as early as 18 August, saying the Allies have 'the cause of progress, peace & civilisation against militarism & despotism'. From this starting point, sentiments harden as German actions are reported. On 28 August, Mabel wrote:

> Many atrocities are reported of the Germans, who seem to have lost all humane feelings. They are said (by a woman who fled from the village [in Belgium]) to have fastened down the mines, where miners were at work, so that the unfortunate men must have died of hunger or suffocation.

Mabel takes the reports of German atrocities very seriously and wholeheartedly, never once contrasting them with the people she had known when she had lived in Heidelberg. For this to happen, she either genuinely felt that the Germany she had known was capable of such barbarity, or she took the reports of atrocity as an authority, indicating the importance of such reports up and down the nation.

The degree of German brutality was greatly contested but just because something was used for propaganda does not mean it did not take place. At the dawn of the twentieth century, Germany had Europe's principal professional army and her militarism treated war as a professional's preserve. Consequently, German military leaders were terrified of civilian or guerrilla resistance, as this flew in the face of the kind of war they wanted to fight. Germany had experienced such resistance in the Franco-Prussian war over Alsace-Lorraine (1870–71), where menacing Francs-tireurs (civilian shooters) proved difficult to deal with. This memory lived on and worried German strategists who felt that the best way to manage the danger was to treat all civilian resistance as a military threat and supress it accordingly. What this translated into has been codified by recent research. In the three months from the start of the war, during the invasion of Belgium, Germans killed some 6,500 civilians, destroyed over 20,000 buildings, raped and used civilians as human shields.[2] Certain events stood out as great losses to Mabel, who wrote on 30 August that: 'Yesterday came the dreadful news that Lorraine had been burnt down & utterly destroyed. It was the principal seat of learning in the Low Countries, with a beautiful Gothic Cathedral, a fine University & a Library of 70,000 volumes. All are destroyed ruthlessly'. She went on to explain that this was due to the German paranoia of Belgian militia who the Germans had 'disarmed long before'. The sense of barbarity against civilians coming from the repercussions of this attack is clear to Mabel: 'Some of the men were shot, some taken prisoners, all turned out of their homes & women & children thrown into trains & taken no one knows where. Never, says the "Times" was there a more horrible crime committed, even in the days of Attila the Hun'.

The treatment of civilians, especially women and children, must not be forgotten or, worse, dismissed because it was used for propaganda. It mattered to the war effort and to people like Mabel that *any* of these things took place. They should matter to us, not only in their own right, but also because they animated Mabel and her generation to respond to them.

The Allies

Given the need to manage morale in war, the main gap between the reports Mabel takes as fact and the known historical reality is the performance of the Allies. Time and again, Mabel gives the impression, or reports as fact, that the Allies are doing exceptionally well or making great gains, when we now know just how touch-and-go the early battles were and just how close it came to a different situation. One of Mabel's first references to Allied progress reports that 'There is no very exciting news', but goes on to say that the enemy are being defeated 'where ever they meet'. Mabel is writing during the early stages of the Battle of the Frontiers, which took place over August and September 1914. Despite being fiercely contested, and successfully halting the Germans from advancing as far as Paris, this was in fact a desperate effort to stem the German advance and one that failed to effectively reverse it. Yet Mabel reiterates a potent sense of coming victory two days later, saying 'all the news so far is good' as the enemy 'are being drawn back on all sides in the small encounters'. She records that 'America is warmly in favour of our cause' when President Woodrow Wilson declared official neutrality on 4 August and the nation took three years, along with several major events, to come in on one side. This impression of good news helps us appreciate how the war was viewed in its infancy, illustrating the context behind the rush of some volunteers in Britain. If it was understood that the Allies were winning every single battle and that all the news was favourable, along with knowing that the war was of paramount importance, then it is unsurprising that some were keen to get in on the action before it was all over. What Mabel believed certainly provides insight into the sort of censorship, misinformation and propaganda that existed.

Mabel herself knew that confusion and contradiction were apparent in August 1914. In a passing comment about the defences of the important Belgian city of Namur (which lay in the Germans' path to France) she wrote: 'It is said that 4 of the forts are still holding out, though the Germans declare they have fallen'. It is in Mabel's digestion of the news that we are able to see the subtleties of its reporting and taken meaning. (Indeed, throughout the diary, seeing what Mabel does and does not believe, or even record, is informative in itself.) As is so often, Mabel's entries have more to them than meets the eye; on 28 August 1914, one of the first reflective and downbeat passages begins: 'There is sad news today [...] The Germans massed their troops especially against the English at Cambrai ... & there was a terrible battle'. She then adds rather patriotically 'The British held their own splendidly & did not allow themselves to be overwhelmed in spite of the Germans being 3 to 1 against them' but the most important part of the entry comes at the end, as Mabel concludes 'the English retired a short distance'. Having given the context of overwhelming numbers, pitched particularly against the English, Mabel for the first time mentions retreat – except she does not; instead she uses the term 'retire'. The difference in words is subtle and the meaning of retire may have been different to Mabel and her time but it is worth stressing that variation in language. Mabel is almost certainly talking about the Battle of Le Cateau, which took place two days earlier and was near Cambrai. The Battle of Le Cateau was a bitterly contested German victory, ending with a tactical British retreat.

What makes the retreat significant is that it was part of a wider withdrawal now known as the Great Retreat, a series of movements into France after the battle on Mons. In fact, the battle had been an effort to slow this general retreat and buy more time for the withdrawing forces, by holding up the Germans. There is a great deal of truth in what Mabel reports, British troops were heavily outnumbered, fought very well and delayed the Germans for precious hours. Nonetheless, it was part of a general and hazardous effort to stop a retreat turning into a rout. Contrast this with a passage written on 12 September where Mabel talks of the Germans themselves in a 'rout' and that three days later, their retreating army 'are reported to be in a miserable plight, short of ammunition & food'. While there may be some truth in this retreat of German forces, a 'rout' clearly did not take place. From late 1914 the defensive lines along the Western Front remained largely static until 1918.

The gap between Mabel's view and the known historical reality begins to shrink from late 1914 onwards. Her passages become steadily more realistic, giving a clearer picture of the stubbornness the Allies encountered and shedding light on why so little progress was being made by each side. In an entry on 24 September 1914, Mabel wrote of an increasing and uncommon German resistance: 'in spite of furious fighting & many bayonet charges, which the Germans, contrary to their usual practice, have not always fled from, but sometimes returned with equal fury'.

By 4 October, Mabel was starting to capture a real impression of stagnant, frustrated warfare locked in attrition. This scenario is one that we would now identify with the war, but for her it appears to be an unexpected and troublesome development: 'And still, though I write after an interval of 10 days, the Great Battle of Aisne is going on. Still 2 great armies face each other from their entrenchments & now one & now the other gains some slight advantage'. Here Mabel writes of the war in terms we would recognise today, and begins to visualise it as the gridlock it was becoming.

Even with this understanding of the war of attrition, Mabel still wrote entries that played up British success and painted the Germans as the ones who suffered from these new rules of the game, as a passage from 23 October 1914 shows:

Altogether the Allies are holding their own splendidly & it seems almost certain that there will be a general retreat of the enemy before long. They have failed to pierce the Allies' line at any point & their trenches are in a terrible condition. Typhoid & Diarrhoea are rife amongst their troops.

On the whole, the Germans had better trenches than the British and in this way benefited from this defensive warfare. It was Valentine's Day 1915 before Mabel devotes some space to recording the condition of the British trenches, complaining that:

> The trenches have been half full of water & the mud has been so dreadful that officers writing to the Times, say that everything they had on & even their hands are thickly plastered with it. Many of our men get their feet frostbitten with the ice cold water they have to stand in. So that, although there is fighting every day & a daily list of casualties, no large numbers of troops have been sent out.

Mabel's eagerness to understand and follow the war's movements, when set against this backdrop of stagnation, comes out more clearly. By 30 July 1916, Mabel is writing of 'The Big Push' and that the 'British have gained 24 square miles of strongly fortified ground from the Germans in France & continue to advance, in spite of desperate resistance & heavy counter attacks'. In 1914 Mabel had used generic catch-all terms, which indicated that the Allies were winning; here she not only recorded specifics – '24 square miles' – but also gives a context of just how hard this was to gain. In an entry on 29 September, Mabel writes of the new 'surprise on the enemy, by our "Tanks", a form of armoured motor car'. In this passage, Mabel mentions the taking of specific areas ('villages like Combles & Thiepval') and details her understanding of the piecemeal nature of Allied gains against enemy resistance, having to go 'through gunfire & bullets & wire' in order to take these villages 'which are really fortresses'. As the war progressed, the gap between Mabel's understanding of it and the reality shrank. This gap tells a fascinating story of the ongoing censorship and propaganda, which ran against the growing detail of news reports and the insight from her brothers in action. Mabel gradually gains a clearer picture of the performance of the Allies and the conditions in which they operated against an enemy she increasingly came to know. It was always to be the case that the war recorded by Mabel was not the one that took place but, as time went on, the two versions began to look more similar. This understanding must have played a significant part in her growing disengagement with the lengthening war. As she came to know it, she grew weary of it and all the harsh realities it brought about.

Figure 8: Recruitment poster from 1917, calling for women to enter uniformed service. (*Royal Pavilion & Museums Brighton & Hove*)

Chapter 3

Roles Vanished, Roles Remade

'Crichton: My lady, I am the son of a butler and a lady's-maid – perhaps the happiest of all combinations, and to me the most beautiful thing in the world is a haughty, aristocratic English house, with everyone kept in his place. Though I were equal to your ladyship, where would be the pleasure to me? It would be counterbalanced by the pain of feeling that Thomas and John were equal to me.'

The Admirable Crichton (a play by J.M. Barrie) 1902

Servants no more

The past is a foreign country, and not always one we would like to visit. Yet the Edwardian era has long held a special place in British memory. Among the first generation to look back on that era, former Prime Minister Harold Macmillan captured one of the lasting sentiments of the time: 'For those of us who remember it, the Edwardian summer was an Indian summer, the last 'warm spell' of Victorian Pax Britannica before the First World War engulfed all and almost destroyed our generation'.[1] The popularity of television shows such as Downton Abbey highlight our sustained interest in Mabel's very different world.

One of the profound effects of the war was the decline of domestic service. While it is easy to overstate this trend, the war did require men for the front, so the economy did restructure to account for that loss of labour. As one solution to this loss, women filled jobs previously held by men. The increase in opportunities for women resulted in fewer of them working in domestic service. This change, amplified by the men who had left domestic service to fight, put a premium on those who remained servants and made keeping such servants more costly to finance. Mabel's diary captures this trend; it begins in a household with a driver and a few servants. The fact that there are servants when the family's wealth does not seem obvious indicates how common the employment of domestic servants was. Imeson was the driver of the family's 1904 Daimler car and, as the only male servant, was unsurprisingly the first to leave. Henry described Imeson as a fairly bad driver with little real understanding of cars.

In spite of his poor driving skills, Mabel writes on 30 November 1914 that 'Imeson has joined the Army Service Corps as Motor Ambulance Driver'. There was clearly support from the family for this move, as 'Henry promised to get Col. Sharpe to write or telephone to have Imeson as driver for one of their 7 Ambulance Motors'. There is an eagerness to help Imeson secure a good role in the army. Painting a potent image, Mabel records that Imeson's last act for the family was to put into storage the car that he drove for them: 'He & Henry have tucked up the car or whatever is necessary for its long rest. How long? I wonder'.

The decline of domestic service over the course of the war was not always as dramatic as a driver leaving early on to join up. When Evans, the family's maid and 'devoted & faithful servant for 22 years', leaves on 23 June 1915, Mabel records the personal loss both to her and the family ('We shall miss her terribly') and that this loss was an inevitability, owing more to time than the war. If anything, the war only prevented a replacement for Evans being found rather than producing any pressure for her to leave. Still, the departure of a servant, an increasingly scarce resource, was given much attention by Mabel, who wrote that she was 'quite alone in the house' as the rest of the servants went to see Evans off. The strain of Evans' retirement is brought up again on 27 June when Mabel wrote 'A great loss! I am dusting the drawing room every morning to try & do with only 2 maids'.[2] The fact that Mabel takes to her diary to complain of the housework she is now having to undertake and the difficulty of having only two maids says more in its seriousness than anything else. Mabel's frustration at having to absorb housework illustrates her expectation of a life free from various domestic duties.

It is no bad thing to remind ourselves that there was, for a great deal of time, a class of people in Britain who had no need to learn to cook, master driving, wash their clothes, lay their table or to do anything meaningful to clean and make presentable the house they lived in. Furthermore, this class extended beyond the super-rich owners of stately homes to people like Mabel, a family living off a modest inheritance and a doctor's salary. It is equally, if not more, important to remind ourselves that there was a class whose function in society extended little beyond those mundane, routine and utterly domestic tasks, paid to support another family's life.

The flavour of such a relationship and the society in which it existed, where position and breeding were in competition with talent and merit, were captured particularly well by the quotation at the beginning of this section from *The Admirable Crichton*, a comic play written in 1902 by J.M. Barrie (the author of *Peter Pan*). The play opens with an awkward social experiment: the family of the house entertain the servants, each side experiencing their new positions with equal horror. In opposition to this experiment, the reader is told that Crichton (the head butler) is 'devotedly attached to his master, who, in his opinion, has but one fault, he is not sufficiently contemptuous of his inferiors'. During the gathering Crichton says 'I'm ashamed to be seen talking to you, my lady' and says that social mixing 'disturbs the etiquette of the servants' hall. After last month's meeting the pageboy, in a burst of equality, called me Crichton. He was dismissed'. Ironically, later on in the play when the family are all wrecked on a desert island, it is Crichton who leads them. Whilst Barrie's play is a comedy, it was only because this structure was so familiar that it could be satirised.

Another great Edwardian writer, H.G. Wells, explored the embarrassment and difficulty of crossing class boundaries in his 1905 work *Kipps: The Story of a Simple Soul*, which sees a new-money story take a turn when the (previously working-class) hero finds his first love as a servant. Kipps embodied the cultural difficulty of climbing the social ladder: '"I'm a regular fish out of water with this money. When I got it – it's a week ago – reely I thought I'd got everything I wanted. But I dunno what to do." His voice went up into a squeak. "Practically," he said, "it's no good shuttin' my eyes to things – I'm a gentleman".'

Having servants was not confined to the Edwardian era. Domestic service was a prevalent feature in British life for some centuries – only leaving the nation in the degree and manner with which it had existed before the war, in the era under the conflict's long shadow. The longevity of domestic service makes its eventual end all the more important. As servants left, so went the lifestyle they supported. It is clear that Mabel struggled with the loss of servants in the Goode household and felt that the subsequent change in her fortunes was worthy of diary space. While not every departure was explicitly linked to the war, the lack of servants was something Mabel deemed noteworthy and an effect she felt.

War work

Mabel was not one of the new generation of women munition workers or service volunteers (see figure 8). Nonetheless, her diary does demonstrate that this middle-class woman was doing hard physical work for the first time in her life for the war effort. The first sign of Mabel lending a hand comes just three days after she started the diary: 'I spent some time this afternoon making a top for a camp stool I have promised for the St John's Ambulance Hospital here'. It was a little over a month after the declaration of war that she first records doing something to support the troops directly, writing on 6 September that 'At Fyling Hall we all knitted socks most industriously for the soldiers'. It is rather a powerful image, a group of women in a provincial city coming together to knit socks energetically for men later to march in them towards the barrels of the enemy's guns.

By 18 March 1915, it is clear that Mabel's role at home had changed too: she picked up as much of Henry's work as she could, at the expense of her personal time:

I have been lazy about writing up my Diary lately, but one good reason has been that I have had to spend every available evening in making out Henry's bills for him. He can come so seldom that I have pressed Evans into service & she has helped me several evenings, then when Henry comes, he only has to send them out.

Not long after this, on 27 April 1915, Mabel responded to national campaigns for help: 'I have got some jute to make sand bags, as the papers say the troops need them by the million'. These activities take on a large role in her life. A few months later on 10 July, Mabel gives a sense of the pressures on her time, as she cuts her entry short with 'now I must mend gloves'.

From this point onwards, Mabel seemed occupied by two projects to support the war effort: haymaking and sandbag production. Entries in late July 1915 captured just how time-consuming this work was. On 22 July, an entry states that for 'Four days I have left at 2.45 & cycled to Skelton, 3 miles, & spent the afternoon making hay' and another on 26 July records that Mabel cycled:

> ... off to Skelton to help Delia with her haymaking. She is alone in charge of the farm, as her brother Arthur is in the A.S.C. in France. Of course all the young labourers are gone too. She has 3 "Patriotic" Lady workers staying in the house & helping her, 2 for wages, 1 for nothing. Of course she is glad of any extra help. I stay till about 7.

This last entry makes it all too clear that middle-class women were obliged by patriotism to step in to do the work traditionally done predominately by men. The war revealed a new need for women, new roles for them and a new chance for them to make their mark in those roles. Mabel adds to the point in an entry on 22 August, writing that 'Last Friday the last load [of hay] was loaded by little Henry! 6 years old, so short of workers were we at the end!' Again, haymaking is quite physically demanding, laborious work; middle-class Mabel (forty-three by this time) would have been out of place doing this work pre-war, to say the very least. The conflict brought her into working life but far more importantly, into what was understood as 'man's work' – something new; something that contributed to the war, and something patriotic.

The same entry also records how Mabel joined other women to support the troops: 'Last Monday & Tuesday Mrs Mends began a series of Working Parties from 2.30–6 to make Sandbags. She has 2,000, & wants 3,000 more to make up 5,000 to send to the W. Riding Division.' This is a fascinating insight into voluntary work undertaken by women to help the war effort. Organised by a woman, Mrs Mends, this project had a serious production target of 5,000 for the local Division and a clear hierarchy modelled on a factory. Mabel makes it plain that she only did this because 'it was too rainy for haymaking'. It is clear that there were many opportunities for work and she had several war-related demands on her time (something which also helps explain why her diary entries became sparser as time went on). We know that Mabel was one of millions of women working for the war effort, but this particular entry gives an indication of just how encompassing this trend was for her generation, as she finds herself amongst familiar faces when hard at work in a factory:

> I found several friends, Miss Harrison and the 2 Miss Ottleys, the Forbes-Dicks etc. It was a busy scene & we had a number of the poorer women sewing up the bags, as fast as they could be cut out & folded in ready for them. I acted as shopwalker, collecting the finished bags & setting new women on to work, etc. It was tiring

Mabel was among the first generation of British women who could vote in a General Election, but she also witnessed, and arguably even played a part in, the changes that helped bring that about. The war altered what was expected of Mabel and what she could do. As men marched away and new industries required expansion, so Mabel entered new and unknown roles. Mabel's new deployment symbolised her changing role in society and the evolution of women's obligations and privileges. The war transformed the lives of women up and down the country, due to the same reason Mabel gave up the diary: because as a conflict it grew in size, demands and length. While the war's expansion marked an end for the diary it was something of a beginning for women and greatly aided the suffrage cause, contributing to the eventual post-war enfranchisement of half of the British adult population.

Figure 9: Recruitment poster from 1914, referencing the Scarborough bombardment which Mabel records. (*Royal Pavilion & Museums Brighton & Hove*)

Chapter 4

Total War

'The war against the civil population of an enemy has been brought to
a fine art by the Germans'

The Times, 17 December 1914

The First World War has often been called the first ever 'total war' – that
is to say, a war which is so encompassing that it demands full deployment
of a nation to the war effort. Importantly, war becomes 'total' when the
distinction between civilian and combatant breaks down. This is achieved
through an economy geared for war, mass mobilisation of troops, and a
heavy use of propaganda to justify the new demands on citizens. Typically,
one nation seeks to destroy the other state's war economy, which is run by
civilians, and its propaganda treats the enemy as a threat so severe that all its
citizens are fair game.

The Second World War is a clear example. States such as Britain went into
great debt to fund fighting, moving from a relatively free economy to a much
more socially disciplined war economy, mobilising masses of troops, making
extensive use of propaganda, bombing civilian cities (Dresden, Hamburg
etc.) and had its own civilian cities bombed (London, Coventry etc). In
short, it was a brutal and all-encompassing struggle; a war so important that
it demanded every effort that could be given to it. The First World War fits
some of these categories, and one of the clearest pictures the diary paints is
that Mabel, and women like her, experienced a new kind of war; a war that
came to them.

Civilians in the line of fire

Unlike previous wars within Mabel's living memory, during the First
World War, British civilians died directly at the hands of the enemy on

British soil. Yorkshire was one of the main areas to suffer from German attacks, due to its lack of naval defences and ease of access from German bases. Just ten days after the outbreak of war, Mabel highlighted the extent to which an invasion was feared when she wrote of the preparations against an enemy invasion: 'On our East coast no lights are allowed at night in windows facing the sea & they are digging trenches along the coast, certainly at Hull'. Again, on 27 November 1914, Mabel captured the fear of potential invasions, writing that a 'German invasion is much talked of & trenches & wire entanglements are I believe made all along the East Coast. I should like to see them'. On 10 December, Mabel gives an account of seeing 'sandbags across the main street going down to the sea, about 3/4 of the way down, with loop holes to fire though' and trenches which 'were rather disappointing'.

Six days later on 16 December 1914, the war's first major attack on British soil took place, as Scarborough and other coastal areas were bombarded by the German Navy. The shocking nature of the event naturally meant Mabel devoted a lot of space to recording it (as did the recruitment campaigns, see figure 9). She wrote on the day of the attack that 'inhabitants fled & are still fleeing to York & Leeds, many of them in their night attire'. The utter unfamiliarity and bewilderment of the civilians with the sights and sounds of war can be seen later on in the passage, when Mabel wrote that a 'lady described the noise of the bursting shells' as 'a hundred thunderstorms rolled into one'. On an entry on 27 December, Mabel extensively records her visit to Scarborough and the site of the attack, writing that:

> Several of the hotels & many private houses along the sea front had all their windows broken & many great gaping holes in them. The low, one-storied restaurant in front of the Grand Hotel was a wreck, every great pane of glass gone & a mass of debris & fallen masonry in the centre, where some people were looking for fragments of shells. One shell had struck the ground below a house & broken the strong iron railing into small pieces, smashed all the windows & bent & twisted the balcony 2 stories above. The train returning was crammed, largely with Scarboro' people fleeing, in case of another bombardment, they said a

despatch rider has come in to say that the Germans would be back in 2 hours.

Here was a civilian, unaccustomed to the destructive power of war, able to see with her own eyes the damage inflicted by the Germans, the victims they created and the fear they struck. Mabel could now feel personally hurt by the war.

The only way to get a person to care for a cause or a project is to make it matter to them. That is why propaganda is so important to the war effort. Outrages, potent images and tales of heroism all help people to connect to the cause of the war, they unify people so that they have a common goal to back and work harder to achieve it (as figures 7, 9, 24, and 43 all show). Mabel was in the first wave of British citizens for generations (probably since the 1745 Jacobite rebellion or even the Civil War period of 1642–1660) to see the damage caused by the enemy first-hand. Having seen this damage, the war meant more to her; she could write on it with more authority, had more reason to act on it and could feel she was a part of it.

What Mabel witnessed also forged her vision of the enemy. The Germans' murder of civilians was seen as a mark of their barbarism. Such outrages were used in several recruitment posters, for instance, urging men to 'remember Scarborough' as in figure 9. The sinking of the passenger ship the Lusitania on 7 May 1915 was another great shock to the Allies, and something Mabel records to have led to 'many anti-German riots' with German 'shops wrecked & large numbers of the enemy aliens... [being] interned'. To kill civilians from different nations, some of which were neutral, as with the sinking of the Lusitania was something Mabel felt no civilised nation would do. She was not alone in that sentiment, as the sinking of the Lusitania would later be credited with helping bring America into the war. Again, posters (and even an innovative animation[3]) were made to compel people to avenge such an act. The German actions against ordinary civilians like Mabel helped to harden public opinion against them.

War in the air

Yet it was the Zeppelin attacks which really exposed civilians to the war. The attacks on the coast and on passenger ships affected those who lived in certain areas, or dared to travel by sea; the nature of aerial attacks meant that anyone could be a target. Early on in the war, on 10 October 1914, and with a note of disapproval at the reaction to it, Mabel picked up on the first mention of an attack by air: 'London has been warned by the authorities not to show any lights except those necessary to direct the traffic. In spite of the warning some of the large shops have meanly tried to attract customers by keeping their lights on as usual'. At this stage, the actual threat of war from the air – something Britons had never experienced before – seemed not to have been fully understood. Yet, Mabel firmly believes that attacks on civilians will take place, saying in the same passage that 'there is no doubt that the Germans intend attacking England & London in particular with their Zeppelins'. The sense that civilians were under threat is captured perfectly in an entry on 19 February 1915 as 'All over England we are more or less expecting Zeppelins'. Mabel gave an insightful impression as to what this meant in practice:

> At all street corners are hung up placards shewing [sic] the different shapes of Germans & English airships & aeroplanes. I have bought one also & hung it up outside the drawing room. People have been warned in the papers to seek refuge in their cellars or the nearest house, if they are out of doors. We propose going into our basement. But I think York is as safe a place as any.

Totally unprecedented, Mabel's extract above emphasises that there was a tangible need to inform and warn citizens about the appearance of enemy weapons and the protection measures against them. The need is made crystal clear in an entry on 21 January 1915 when Mabel wrote of an air raid, commenting that the 'places chosen for attack were, as usual, undefended'. Yet, rather curiously for the reader, she adds later on how unfazed she is by this new threat, commenting that the latest attacks 'shews how little real danger is to be feared from them'. Nonetheless, Mabel clearly felt that the

Germans had a monopoly on attacking non-combatants and that this set them apart in the war:

> The Americans can see what the Germans appear unable to, the difference between dropping bombs on airship sheds & arsenals & military stores, as the Allies' airmen do, & dropping them on harmless people, including women & children & private property. There are great rejoicings in Germany at the cowardly attack by their pet Zeppelins.

The First World War opened up Britain's skies to the will of the enemy. With this, the war came home to Mabel. The first personal threat from Germany is recorded by Mabel on 16 April 1915: 'we had our first Zeppelin alarm', describing the siren as a 'weird, penetrating sound' and making it clear that it took them some time to decipher the noise. This first encounter took an unexpected turn when a young couple sought to seek shelter, as the woman had been in the Scarborough attacks which 'had made her nervous'. The second visit came on 11 August when Mabel wrote: 'Yesterday we heard that the Zeppelins had attacked the East Coast and come as near York as Selby. Some people in York were awakened by the noise … The fire engines were got ready & the hooter was very nearly sounded'. Not long after on the 22nd of August another attack is mentioned: 'There have been several Zeppelin raids on the East Coast. No places are mentioned in the papers, but privately I hear … 30 people were injured, but none killed'.

It was on 2 May 1916 that Mabel really experienced the menace of the Zeppelins, as recorded on the following day's entry. Mabel 'was just reading Prayers (10 pm) when the gas went down & got so low, I had to guess the words at the end. I looked out & found the street in darkness & the trams stopped running'. (This lowering of the gas was the customary warning given by the city, rather than air raid sirens which it was feared would help the Zeppelin pilots know where to bomb.)[4] Mabel, having 'thought it very likely they would not really come over York' started to make preparations for an attack before listening out to hear 'the loud thud-thud of the great engines, apparently passing overhead'. Aware of what this meant, she and her servant Price sought cover but 'before we got in, Crash! The bombs began to fall. Several loud ones made the back door rattle & shake & alarmed Price a good deal'.

The extract goes on to describe that 'Presently we heard the fire engines tearing by, a motor one & a horse one, galloping'. The morning after the attack, Mabel was able to see the damage wrought by the enemy with her own eyes, as she 'cycled round & looked at the wrecked homes' saying 'Many are wrecked in various parts of York & very sad to see'. In this extract Mabel makes a point of where the bombs fell, saying 'Nearly all are little two storey houses' and, almost as if it were a consolation, 'No damage was done to any other large building of importance'. The damage wrought by these bombs is telling in itself of this new type of warfare: even when they wanted to, the Zeppelins would struggle to hit 'buildings of importance', making the killing largely indiscriminate. Ordinary little houses – family homes – were being bombed. Mabel, though a woman at home, was in the firing line. The war must have felt a great deal closer that morning.

It was on 20 August 1916 that Mabel first records spotting a Zeppelin: that novel and ominous enemy machine. The passage starts with Mabel waking up to hear 'distant crashes'. Something, which could be taken as a sign of her growing familiarity with attacks, leads her to immediately think of Zeppelins. After listening out to confirm this, Mabel then goes to hear the battle rage between the home defences (recently installed at the edge of the city following the destruction of the first attack)[5] and the attacker by the window. 'For ½ an hour or so, the booms & crashes came at intervals. Then came several crashes, followed by Pop! Pop! "Anti-Aircraft guns" I thought'. Things took a turn when Mabel noticed 'a steady humming, growing quickly louder'. Realising that the Zeppelin was coming closer, Mabel went out to see what she could see:

> It was a still, starlight night. The humming had become a loud throbbing & up there, showing against the stars, was the long, black, threatening shape of the Zeppelin. It was a most thrilling, weird sensation, standing out there by myself & watching it approaching rapidly. … the Zepp passed, apparently exactly overhead. I gazed at it & prayed a silent prayer that it might not drop a bomb just then.

There Mabel was, a woman born in 1872, standing directly under a German airship praying it would not kill her. The danger was very real, as Mabel went on to write 'A few minutes after it got out of sight, we heard several bombs dropped'.

The final raid in the diary suggests both how accustomed the household was becoming to these raids and just how terrifying they could be. Mabel writes of the early warning she received 'Our warning (gas turned low) came at 10.45. The two maids, Price & Kathleen & I went below, in our coats. I heard the throb of the engines from the scullery door & just afterwards the bombs began to fall'. The passage continues:

> It was very alarming & disagreeable, as we had to be quite in the dark. Kathleen told her beads fervently,[6] while I held on to Rex & suppressed his indignant barks by holding his mouth to.

The above passages highlight the way in which the threat of death, at the hands of the enemy, repeatedly loomed over Mabel. More importantly, the passages illustrate how novel and extraordinary these raids were at the start of the war, how grimly familiar they became in such a short space of time and how they never lost their terror. The fear was justified. Mabel was far from alone in experiencing air raids and for some, the attacks came too close; mainland Britain had over 4,000 casualties across the course of the war.[7]

A little over ten years after the first powered flight, war was being waged in the air. In an all-out war between major powers, we would now expect all our lives to be under threat. It is taken as a given that military power has developed to reach and terrorise civilian targets. The sky now acts as the main channel by which one nation can inflict harm on another – this was the first time that channel had opened.

Hunger as a weapon: the power of food

It is said that truth is the first casualty in war, but in this war it had a companion: as truth crept out, it seems that hunger crept in. A hallmark of total war is the erosion of distinctions between the civilian economy and the war economy. When the war effort is all-consuming it requires the broad mobilisation of people's strength, silver and spirit. Destroying an enemy increasingly becomes a question of damaging the civilian economy and the civilian morale that underpins the war effort.

A crucial part of that economy and morale is the food supply. A sufficient and sustained food supply is vital for political stability and an advanced civilisation. In order to have an advanced civilisation and a copious food supply there needs to be a specialisation in the economy. We do not all toil on the land, rather one group produces an abundance and from that others, not concerned with producing food, can be doctors, economists, industrial engineers, musicians, tailors etc. This structure creates an intrinsic vulnerability for that civilisation, because the specialised food-producing group must provide in abundance, and the produce must be distributed to the wider population. There is a correlation between serious, sustained and widespread political instability and a poor and threatened food supply. The Spanish novelist Cervantes alluded to this when he wrote 'all sorrows are less with bread';[8] a meagre food supply can amplify existing sorrows and create new ones.

Such was the thought-process behind the blockade policy that Britain imposed on Germany for the duration of the war. Starting in August 1914, Britain wanted to starve German industry of the raw materials and imports it needed, with the intention of weakening the military forces that those industries supported. Going further than this, there was also a deliberate policy to restrict and manage the food imports that Germany received and the fertilisers used to bolster German agriculture. All this meant that the German population was increasingly cut off from the outside world, and that their economy had to move towards self-sufficiency. As the economy struggled to meet the needs of the population, restrictions and innovations were put in place. Bread rationing was established as early as 1915 and, according to one estimate, there was a fifty per cent increase in the cost of feeding a family between 1914 and 1915.[9] Germany's 'war bread', the hated *Kriegsbrot* or 'K-Brot', began to symbolise the sub-standard replacements in a 'make do economy', because it contained ingredients such as dried potatoes and pulverised straw.

In the early years of the conflict Britain could have, but did not, succumb to her vulnerabilities and become obliged to adapt and make do. On 14 August 1914, shortly after the outbreak of war, Mabel alludes to the idea that the war has the potential to starve civilians but makes it clear that this is unlikely: 'There seems no great danger of a famine at present, as our trade routes from Canada and America are being well protected by Cruisers & there are only 5 German Cruisers trying to intercept the vessels'. In an entry the following day, Mabel records the feeling of national vulnerability in the news, as 'The papers have been recommending everyone who has a little ground to use it for planting vegetables in, as they may be wanted later on'. In a revealing response with what proved a misguided belief, Mabel commented: 'It seems rather farfetched, as we grow most of our fresh vegetables in England, I should think, but we are going to plant a few in a corner of the garden, where the grass is poor & should be dug up anyhow'. This was just as well because by 1916 the war had forced the British state – for the first time in its history – to start rationing. That is, to directly manage distribution of food, as the food supply was deemed too meagre to risk a hands-off approach by the Government.

As the Germans suffered from restrictions on importing food, so they retaliated by trying to blockade Britain. Lacking a navy powerful enough to defeat Britain outright, the Germans relied on cruisers to pick off merchant ships before turning to submarine or U-Boat warfare. Mabel first mentions the effects of a potential blockade on imports when she records price increases, which she does three times in the diary: on 15 August 1914, 14 February 1915 and 10 December 1916. Mabel only gives this her detailed attention in the entry for 14 February saying: 'Prices are going up. Flour is 48/ – a sack or 50/ & coal is 35/ – 39/ a ton instead of 15/ – 19/ a ton'. These efforts to wage war on the food supply brought the conflict into the home via the purse and the kitchen table (an obvious talking point worthy of illustration, as displayed by the new jokes and attitudes shown in figures 10–12). The war visibly changed not only what went onto people's plates, but also what people saw of the effort to secure food beyond the land. Mabel highlighted her awareness of this effort when she recorded on 26 May 1915: 'Such a calm & peaceful sea today, only the inevitable mine sweepers at work to remind one of the dreadful conflict raging but a short distance away'.

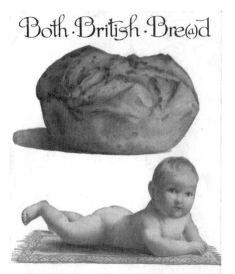

Figures 10–12: Postcards showing the shortages and scarcities the war brought to the Home Front, especially the staples such as coal and bread. (*Tony Allen's WWI Postcard Collection*)

Yet even as Mabel recorded the rise in food prices, she contrasted the situation favourably with Germany. In the same entry as above, she wrote that 'there is no scarcity of food, as there is in Germany, where the Government have taken over the food supplies & only allow ½ lb of flour per head a day. They issue bread tickets'. She adds that this war on merchant ships expands the parameters of the war and 'is rather cutting their own throats, as now the Allies can seize all vessels carrying foodstuffs to Germany, as being for the Government & therefore for military purposes, whereas before private German firms could not be prevented from having food brought them'. Seeing this struggle as a part of the war, Mabel felt that Britain was at an advantage. Britain certainly was.

Price rises stemming from the German retaliation to the blockade represented the genuine and deadly struggle to ensure food arrived at Britain. When Mabel wrote of the war on food imports on 18 February 1915 she gave it serious attention, explaining: 'I must write a few lines today, as this day begins the German submarine attacks against English food supplies. They have threatened to torpedo all our merchant vessels & also neutral ones, which are bringing us supplies'. She adds just how futile these attacks are, as 'The traders & shipping people are taking it quite calmly & insurance rates have not gone up. But rewards are offered for any vessels which sink or ram or give warning about submarines of the enemy'.

For comparison, Mabel later mentions the situation in Germany, as English prisoners were exchanged and reported that they were 'very badly fed', given 'food which in England would be given to the pigs & not even enough of that & if they complained, they were told that "you are starving us"'. Mabel makes it clear that they 'are undoubtedly short of food supplies'. As the diary goes on, it reveals that Britain was not all that far behind Germany. On 30 May 1915 Mabel recorded pre-rationing attempts to make best use of the food coming into the country and her adherence to them: 'There has been an appeal issued, asking people not to eat much meat, as the supply is less than usual & it is important to save milk for the children. We are just having it once, in the middle of the day here'. One potent comment 'we are feeling the shortage of food', at the very end of the diary, gives an impression of the effect the war had on British stomachs and provides a contrast with the confidence in the food supply Mabel had at the war's outset.

There is a crippling aim to the politics of hunger. As the war lengthened and accordingly grew in scope in an effort to shorten itself, it was increasingly fought through hunger, attempting to starve an economy and weaken its people. Post-Agricultural-Revolution Britain had no divine right to be free of famine. It was hardly inevitable that Mabel would not write of real hunger. Britain and Mabel did experience price rises, efforts to limit and manage consumption, campaigns to 'grow your own food' and, eventually, rationing. Naval superiority ensured that German efforts did not have an even greater effect.

In contrast, the Allied Blockade effectively forced the German state to manage the existing food supply and create supplements and substitutes to maintain the best possible calorie level for its citizens. The German winter of 1916–17, known as the Turnip Winter, makes it clear just how hard this task was as the war went on. The fragile and poorly managed food supply was hit by the failure of potato crops and turnips were virtually the only substitute left. Ultimately, however, these efforts failed to prevent starvation. Statistics around the exact number of Germans who starved to death as a result of the blockade are notoriously hard to calculate and rely upon. Disease and poor diet probably worked together to cause death, while cold and fatigue must have been factors in some fatalities. Add to this layering of causes the fact that authorities recording deaths at the time were far from independent. Despite this, it is worth mentioning that German accounts calculated that between 700–800,000 civilians died due to the blockade and even a more conservative estimate by J. Winter still put the number at over 470,000.[10] The war was a total war; a war that proved inescapable for civilians; a war waged against nations, not just their armies.

The civilian suffering (and even casualties) experienced by Germany allude to what life could have been like had Mabel been on the other side of the war. Yet in every European nation, there is evidence of how profoundly the war affected civilian life. Through Mabel's entries, the above shows the ways in which this war changed what civilians thought, did, and lost for the cause. To Mabel, these developments were entirely unexpected intrusions into her comfortable Edwardian life. They were intrusions which resulted from a war that had not only evolved into a new and terrible type of conflict but had also lengthened beyond all but the most prescient expectations – a war that put an end to the hopes of millions of bright-eyed young men as much as it put out the glittering lamps of Imperial Europe.

Figure 13: The Diarist, Mabel Goode, circa 1904.

Chapter 5

About the Diarist

Mabel Goode was the third and youngest child of Dr Henry and Mary Goode (neé Dunnicliff). Mabel's parents married in 1867, when Henry was aged 47 and Mary was 25. They lived at 27 Friar Gate, Derby, where they started a family. Mabel was born into relative affluence and a solidly middle-class social position. Henry was a doctor, working as a surgeon and general practitioner, and Mary's family were also comfortably off – her father was once the Mayor of Derby.

The three children were born in quick succession. Stuart, the eldest, on 7 July 1869 and Henry just over a year later on 10 September 1870, followed by Mabel within two years, born on 27 September 1872. Within six months, Mabel's mother had died – not during childbirth but following complications from it, leaving a 3-year-old, a 2-year-old and a 6-month-old to look after. Her father, needing someone to help him care for his young family, rapidly remarried in 1874 and Mabel's step-mother, Emma Goode, is the 'mother' to whom she refers in her diary.

Having lost her mother at the start of her life, Mabel again experienced bereavement at the age of 7 when her father died in 1879. It is hard to tell what effect this had on Mabel and her brothers. Emma never re-married and, while Mabel is clearly close to her step-mother, the role Emma played in raising the children single-handedly and the decisions she made led to Henry remarking in later life that he was 'dragged up rather than brought up'.

A Briton in Germany – but no Germany in the Briton

Shortly after both Mabel's biological parents died, her step-mother decided to move the family from Derby to Germany. According to family accounts, the reason for this was to soothe Henry's 'weak chest' with the cleaner air found there. From 1881 until 1887 the family lived in Neuenheim, a suburb of the ancient university city of Heidelberg (see figure 15 for a painting of the house in Neuenheim). Some family records are inevitably lost to time, but what is certain is that Mabel's later childhood and early teenage years were spent in Germany and that she had a German schooling. (One picture of the children in Heidelberg exists, see figure 14.) It is known that both the brothers could speak German and it is reasonable to assume Mabel could too.

This meant that at the outbreak of war, Mabel and her brothers, unlike many other Britons, saw Germany not as a country of which they had little direct knowledge but as a place where they had lived, studied in and called home. Living in a university town in particular, German cultural heritage must have been something with which all three young people were very familiar. This was an age when some had called Germany the land of poets and thinkers (*Das Land der Dichter und Denker*, a term coined in 1836). Intellectual and literary giants such as Goethe, Schiller, Hegel, Schopenhauer, Marx, Engels, Nietzsche and Rilke, and the musical heritage of Bach, Mozart, Beethoven, Wagner, Brahms and many more, all ensured that Germany held a special place in European culture throughout the nineteenth and early twentieth century. In Britain, of course, the monarchy historically has had close ties with Germany and Queen Victoria had chosen as her consort the German Prince Albert. Many upper and middle-class British children might have had German tutors and would have been familiar with German music, poetry and the well-known fairy-tales of the Brothers Grimm. Years later, Mabel's brother Henry would grow up to marry Rosetta Shann, a doctor's daughter from York, who had been taught by her German governess in the 1900s to memorise and recite aloud long passages of German epic poetry. The relationship between Germany and Britain before the war may have been competitive but it was often close and mutually appreciative.

Against this backdrop Mabel's upbringing in Germany and her exposure to German culture makes the way she speaks about the country and her acceptance of her former host nation's reported barbarism all the more striking. Early on in the war Mabel easily accepts some of the odder stories about the German leadership, as a passage from 4 October 1914 suggests: 'The German Emperor goes about in a train.... He has his staff with him & a body guard of 10,000 Prussians & a large number of detectives from all parts of Germany. And his movements are kept very secret, the old coward!'

Figure 14: Mabel, Stuart and Henry as children, circa 1883 (taken in Heidelberg).

Figure 15. The Goode residence in Neuenheim, Heidelberg.

The war reports painted a picture of German society and morality that must have been quite unfamiliar with the Germany Mabel had grown to know. Mabel is clearly horrified by the Germans' conduct in war, having written that the Germans 'seem to have lost all humane feeling' (28 August 1914) and 'They really behave more like madmen than a civilised nation' (21 September 1914). As the war progresses Mabel even turns her back on Germany as a whole, as shown in this passage from the 31 March 1915:

> As a rule most of the crews have been allowed a few minutes to save themselves, but yesterday a submarine torpedoed the Liner 'Falaba' before passengers & crew had time to get into their boats & the German brutes jeered at the poor struggling creatures drowning in the ice-cold water, about 112 drowned. Such is German Kultur!

It is distinctly odd that not once does the diary give any indication that Mabel knew Germany personally and she never attempts to question war reports or propaganda on the basis that she had known the people and the character of the enemy nation. The fact that the diary is silent on her German experiences is telling of her faith in the war news on Germany. The growing scorn she shows the enemy symbolises the wider break in Anglo-German relations.

To find a home in England and a servant at home

The family left Germany in 1887 because Stuart wanted to join the army. In an anecdote which reveals both the close relationship between Germany and Britain at the time, and the degree of seriousness with which the family took military service, Emma answered Stuart's initial call to join the army by asking him: 'Which one, dear? The German army uniforms look so much better!' In a decision which was to transform their later destinies, the 18-year-old Stuart insisted on the British army and so the family moved back to Britain, settling in number 3 Vicarage Gardens, Kensington.

In Kensington the family took on a new servant, known as Price (it is around this time that figures 16 and 17 were taken). She served Mabel for around forty years and makes regular appearances in the diary. Given that Mabel never married, Price was one of her closest lifelong companions. On

Figure 16: Mabel, Stuart and Henry as adolescents, circa 1888 (taken in Ryde).

Figure 17: Mabel Goode, circa 1889, Kensington.

the 3 May 1916 Mabel wrote that 'I am living home alone & have only Price for my servant' which was to become the norm for a great deal of the later part of her life. The way Mabel speaks of Price in the diary gives a flavour of how servants of such long standing were treated by the last generation that could really expect to have them. For instance, later in the same passage on 3 May 1916, Mabel wrote 'The bombs began to fall. Several loud ones made the back door rattle & shake & alarmed Price a good deal, but she was really very brave & quiet. Rex barked furiously'. A passing comment on 20 August 1916 indicates a real concern for Price: 'I called gently to Price, in case she was awake & frightened'. Indeed, as the diary goes on it mentions Price more and more, indicating that the relationship between Mabel and Price grew closer as the toils of war increased. The cost of the war meant households had fewer servants, shrinking in size as men went off to fight. Servants also remained employed into older age due to war work drawing in the younger generation. The relationship between Mabel and the servants is an interesting side note in the diary but to understand Mabel and the people important to her, it must be appreciated that, in whatever capacity, she shared a great deal of her life with Price in a relationship which was common then but would be deemed archaic now.

Mabel the artist: from her twenties to her forties

Mabel showed enough artistic skill and enthusiasm to gain entry into The Slade School of Fine Art. It is not known when she began her studies there but she finished her course in 1895, when she was 23 years old.

The Slade, in Bloomsbury, was a world-renowned centre for the study of art. Founded at University College London in 1871, it is only one year older than Mabel. It arguably produced some of the most important British artists of the twentieth century and was the first British art school which allowed women to study art on equal terms with men, by permitting women students access to study from life models. Mabel's course would probably have included study from the life model, drawing from the antique and the draped model. Despite the emphasis on life-drawing at the Slade, Mabel does not seem to have been interested in portraying human figures. Her forte was chiefly in picturesque landscapes, such as charming cottages, ruins or seascapes. (See figures 44 and 48 for paintings by Mabel). From her notes and family anecdotes, we know that her interest was in the work of more traditional artists such as John Ruskin (1819–1900) and William Morris (1834–96), a leading member of the Arts and Crafts Movement.

The family may have been able to afford their own horse-drawn carriage, but it is also probable that, to make the regular 3½ mile journey from Kensington to the Slade, Mabel travelled by her own means. Choosing to take a course at the Slade demonstrated an independent spirit at a time when most women of her age would have been expected to be contemplating marriage and child-rearing rather than study. At the Slade, Mabel was able to develop the artistic skills she would put to use for the rest of her life (figure 49 shows her painting in the 1930s). Over time, art came to mean more to her than any other activity and, in later life, Mabel was able to earn her living as a painter.

The move to York, setting the scene

Once Henry had finished studying medicine and came back from the Boer War, he moved in 1904 to buy a practice in York, accompanied by his mother and sister. They were to stay in this house until 1916 when the War Office commandeered it for its use. Mabel's other brother Stuart, meanwhile, is known to have moved to Canada after retiring from the British Army: probably in around 1911–12.

Thus, at the outbreak of the war in 1914, Mabel, Henry and their mother Emma had been living together for ten years in York, at 8 St Leonards. By 1914 Mabel would have been 42 years old and, as far as is known, there had been no proposals of marriage. (See figure 13 for the picture of Mabel taken in the year of the move.) The first entry in the diary (11 August 1914) suggests that the two siblings had established themselves in York's social circles, by recording a visit to 'the Archbishop's Garden Party at Bishopthorpe', and Mabel later mentions various friends in York and elsewhere but overall the impression one gets is of a quiet and somewhat routine life. Her expectation for her future would appear to have been that life would carry on as it was: a medical practice in York, the two siblings and their mother. It is in this setting that the diary opens.

Figure 18: Henry Goode, circa 1889, Kensington.

Chapter 6

The Brothers Goode

Henry

Education

Henry (born 10 September 1870) was the middle of the three children. Of the three, he was the only one to marry and have descendants and thus he is the one we know the most about. Family recollections are that Henry did not speak very fondly of his time in Germany. The main positive anecdote of his time in Heidelberg is a memory of being able to ice-skate for about six weeks of the year. Of all the children, it is likely that Henry came to know Germany best. Family information tells us that he had his first taste of higher education at Heidelberg University. Although, given that he was only 17 years old, it remains unclear in what capacity he was a student.

Taking after his father, Henry's great interest and skill lay in medicine. After his education at Heidelberg, Henry attended the University of London when his family moved back to Britain, matriculating in June 1889 (see figure 18 for a photograph from this year). He trained as a doctor at St Thomas' Hospital and Birkbeck College, London. Henry then went to Edinburgh University to get his surgeon's qualification, the FRCSE.

To War and to practice

Henry's first experience of war was far away from home, in an Imperial conflict. Having qualified as a surgeon, Henry answered the call to the Boer War (1899–1902), serving throughout its duration. Here Henry was one of 200 surgeons recruited for the war and was involved in the early use of X-rays in the field. He was also responsible for distributing pay to the medical staff in his unit. He passed down the story that the food was so hard, and dental hygiene so poor, that some British troops really struggled to eat supplies.

Returning from the Boer War and now in his early thirties, Henry turned to his medical career. At that time a doctor had to buy a practice, and so Henry bought a house at St Leonard's Place, which was known as the 'Harley Street of York'. Quickly put to action, Henry was made the deputy Medical Officer of Health for the City of York during the smallpox epidemic of 1904. As a doctor working well before the foundation of the National Health Service in 1948, this was one of the few occasions Henry worked directly for the government during peacetime. Before the NHS, Henry would have virtually total control over whom he saw and what he did. Charging for services would also be a matter of his own discretion, and there are several items still in the possession of the family that Henry had received as 'thank you' gifts or in lieu of payment. The practice was within the family home, with a waiting room and a consultancy at the front of the house. Work and home life merged and Henry was known to unplug the one telephone in the house every night and take it upstairs with him when he went to bed so he could take emergency calls easily.

And so to the Front

Of all the family, Henry was without doubt the one most involved in the war. Consequently, we have more information on Henry's war and what it was like for him at the Front than anybody else featured in the diary. Throughout the war, Henry was in the Royal Army Medical Corps (RAMC) attached to the 49th (West Riding) Division and was working in a Field Ambulance Station, spending a great deal of time near Ypres. The work of the RAMC revolved around getting wounded troops to dressing stations in order to save lives. In practical terms this entailed setting up and maintaining a casualty evacuation chain, rest areas and sick rooms. Yet the diary gives us a rather chaotic picture of Henry's work and suggests that he undertook a great variety of tasks. In terms of personal risk, Henry not only worked on the wounded soldiers directly in a station, but also assessed the extent of the wounds in the field and helped to bring in the wounded. Mabel makes it clear on 24 September 1914, before Henry leaves for the Front, that the work is dangerous given that 'so many of the R.A.M.C. men are killed, wounded or taken prisoner' due to the work being either in or very close to the action.

Before deployment, Henry's training in England lent insight into preparation for, and attitudes towards, war. The way in which Henry prepared for the war, and his attitude in preparing for the Front, gives this diary the advantage of showing us what the quiet before the storm was like. Henry joined up and waited for orders to leave with some calm and humour. Mabel's first diary entry recorded Henry's initial reaction to England declaring war, saying 'Well, it's good-bye to mufti'.[1] From that moment until departing for the Front, much of Henry's energy was employed in making practical arrangements for the campaign. Henry asked Mabel for an initialled pint mug (13 August 1914) and French and German dictionaries (18 August 1914) and he spent time 'considering how to place an Ambulance body on his Daimler chassis & take it with him to France' (6 October 1914).

In part, the motivation for this careful preparation may lie in the fact that – most interestingly – Henry seemed to go against the 1914 consensus in thinking that the war will last some time. Mabel, possibly rather dismissively, writes on 12 September 1914 that:

> Henry, who was here yesterday, speaks of it lasting a year, but I think the wish is father to the thought, as it seems his Brigade are quite likely to go to the front & he is anxious for the war to last, or rather, to get out before the war ends.

It appears both that Henry had some insight into the scale of the struggle (he had, after all, previous experience of a debilitating and bloody war) and also that he was anxious to do his bit.

Henry's energy was rewarded when he was promoted from Lieutenant to Captain, announced in the *London Gazette* on 26 February 1915. Recorded the day after, this came as a delightful surprise to Mabel, who wrote proudly, 'Really neither Mother nor I expected he would get it, as the rule is 3½ years as Lieut. before being promoted & even during this war they seem to have kept to the rule & indeed very few R.A.M.C. Captains have been made in any Field Ambulances'. Mabel later adds a back story that it was partly the result of requests for recommendations, 'General Kenny helped him about it, as Major Clyde & Col – sent the papers back & would not recommend him', showing a keen persistence.

Figure 19: Photo taken by Mabel of Henry in 1914.

Newly made a Captain, Henry left for the Front on 13 April 1915. Expressing sentiments which it is easy to imagine were being felt across the nation, Mabel recorded what that day meant to her:

Henry is really gone and to France! It seems difficult to realise that one will never now find his cap & coat hanging up in the hall or flung down in the dining room, when one comes in; that no longer will he come in to tea, bringing us his latest news & sending Rags half wild with delight.

The wider community also felt the apprehension of the men going into danger's way. Mabel recorded on 27 April 1915 that the 'Dean mentioned

TO THE R.A.M.C.

Who are these who go where the bullets fly,
 Where the shells come crashing down,
Where thicker, and thicker, the wounded lie,
 In the ranks of the khaki brown?

All un-armed are they, neither sword nor gun
 Do they bear for defence or hurt.
Then what do they where the ruthless Hun
 Is doing his deadly work?

Though they bear no arms, they are fighting
 a foe,
 Whose touch ends our mortal breath;
Where their comrades are stricken and lying low
 They are waging a war with Death.

Thus they count not their own lives to them
 dear,
 So their comrades' lives be saved,
While they bind up their wounds, and with
 tender cheer,
 Bear them back where the Red Cross waves.

Is not this a Christ-like work to do?
 Can a "greater love" we see?
Then give we honour where honour is due—
 To the men of the R.A.M.C.
                                        M.G.
 8 St. Leonard's, York.

Figure 20: Mabel's poem about the RAMC's work, the only war poem she wrote for which a record of publication exists. Mabel mentioned this in her entry on 9 November 1914: 'I have had my first poem printed 'To the R.A.M.C.' in the Yorkshire Herald of Oct 31st. Certainly war inspires poetry. Nearly every day there is some poem in the Times & in the Yorkshire Herald.'

it last Sunday & asked people to pray for them. The poor old man quite broke down'. By this time the war had already lasted longer than many imagined it would and the scale of the conflict must have been increasingly apparent, as recruitment drive after recruitment drive spread like wildfire across the country. Mabel's entry on 7 May 1915 gives us a good idea of the level of civilian support that troops at the Front could expect and what sort of things they were asking for. Henry's requests for homely items such as 'some tinned things, tongue & sardines & milk & a homemade cake' contrast with letters for vital equipment not adequately being provided by the Government; 'Mother has sent him 2 kinds of respirators to save him from the effects of possible poisonous gases'. Family stories paint a picture of a man acutely aware of the harm to which he was exposing himself. We know that as a doctor Henry had a clear understanding of just how very painful stomach wounds were. Consequently, he used to wear body-armour (as supplied to grenade throwers) over his stomach when exposed to shell-fire, giving us an idea of the extra protection some troops found for themselves.

In the thick of it

When Henry's son was setting off to serve in the Second World War, he asked his father about his experiences in the First World War. Henry had little to say and could not recall much. It seems Henry made no conscious effort to record his war experience. Despite this, a picture can be painted through the diary entries, anecdotes, medal records and objects brought back.

From the start, Henry was put to use to save lives. Mabel gave a sense of this, writing on 16 May 1915 that Henry 'had twice running been up till 2 a.m. attending to the wounded coming in', adding 'he says that last Sunday they had a "big scrap" there & they had to take off their coats & roll up their sleeves & work for all they were worth & that the state of many of the wounded was pitiable & the injuries terrible'. To imagine what was asked of him in those early days of the war and the sheer scale of casualties created by an increasingly industrialised war is not for the faint-hearted. To be the person responsible for patching up these troops, or fighting to keep them alive is a task hard to capture in words. Yet here – and time and time again

– Henry displays his typical British understatement, laconically calling the battle nothing more than a 'big scrap'.

The diary reminds us that Henry was right at the Front. An entry for 16 May shows us just how constant the possibility of death was; Henry was: 'living in an ambulance in a village which is shelled every day. They visit the aid-posts from there every morning & evening, with bullets whizzing & sputtering about them'. Again, in his usual understatement, Henry's only comment is: 'it is very exciting'. Mabel goes on to relate how the fighting became so intense that the medical work had to be halted: 'they often have to stop on the way till things quiet down'. This picture of the ferocity of the fighting and the continual danger is reinforced by an anecdote. On one occasion, Henry and an orderly had rescued a wounded soldier from the front line and were taking him to the casualty station by carrying him between them, one on each side. As they walked along, a shell exploded in front of them and a piece of shrapnel struck and killed the soldier as he was carried between them.

The pressures of Henry's work brought him into the heart of the struggle and kept him there. By 2 June 1915, Mabel could write that Henry 'is sleeping every other night in a shell-swept village ½ a mile from the firing line, does not even remove his boots & gaiters'. One gets an impression of the inexorable nature of the task from Mabel's concern three months, later on 5 September 1915 that 'It is too funny of him not to write'. Enduring such continuous danger for months at a stretch clearly took its toll not only on those participating directly at the front line but on their families too. Mabel's understated remark that it is 'too funny' that she has had no communication from him, hints at the relentless worry she (and their mother) also had to bear.

Mabel's concern for Henry's life is frequently conveyed and well founded. Yet Henry did adapt to his surroundings. He noted that the timing of the German shelling had a pattern to it. If the Germans followed a routine, there were times when it was reasonably safe to collect the wounded. Only so much could be done to minimise risks, however. An entry on 23 June 1915 shows just how touch-and-go the war was for Henry:

His dressing station [was] set on fire by the shells, & the bombs close to it got quite hot & were thrown into a ditch to cool them. His mackintosh in the dressing station was cut to pieces & he has ordered another. He rushed in between the shelling & seized his possessions & the dressings. His map & map case & cover & bicycle were destroyed. After that he had to have his dressing station in a dug out. There the General asked him to go & see where a shell had fallen & no sooner had he got outside than a piece of shell flew towards him & dropped at his feet. He says they fly about for 1 minute after the explosion.

Mabel's description of Henry having to operate in such circumstances, amidst such destruction, is one of the best insights the diary gives into what life at the Front was like.

The entries also give the impression of the comradeship that developed in such trying circumstances. Various entries copy the nicknames Henry uses for his comrades 'Stewey' & 'Hughy' and an entry on 29 October 1916 captured Henry sharing his birthday cake: 'much appreciated in the mess'. The comradeship must have been reinforced by the static and ever-dangerous nature of war and the shortcomings of the wider army to provide supplies, improve conditions or deliver victory. Curiously, Henry seems to hold an unexpected affection for the discomfort and jeopardy of the Front, as Mabel wrote on 23 June 1915 that 'personally he prefers the trenches & sleeps better among the shells!'

The sights Henry saw at war, and the environment he was expected to work in, changed as the nature of the conflict developed. Mabel wrote on 27 September 1915 that Henry wants field glasses 'particularly to observe the aeroplanes with, as he cannot see if they are German or not'. There is a profound significance to this statement: this was written twelve years after the first ever powered flight in recorded human history, yet now Henry is seeing these machines on such a regular basis such that he wants field glasses to check which side they are on so that he can act accordingly.

As the technological race with the enemy put extra burdens on the State to provide for the war effort, so the diary alludes to the fact that the British government was struggling to gear up to the challenge. On 27 September 1915, Henry wrote from the Front that 'the English are very short of ammunition'. The so-called Shell Scandal or Shell Crisis is usually dated from around this time. The crisis was a serious political issue, which eventually helped topple the last purely Liberal government and led to the war effort being managed by a Coalition. The political crisis had military implications; battles such as Neuve Chapelle (10–13 March 1915) are often cited as examples of the desperate lack of shells translating into the British being unable to properly command the field and take advantage of a situation, leading to needless loss of much life.

Put simply, the demands of the war had been totally underestimated. Britain needed more and better equipment for this lengthening war. The minds of the nation had to turn to developing new weapons and machines, while funding had to be found by a government locked into financing a war it had badly misjudged.

From the diary's point of view, the obvious failures in adequately supplying the army did not end after the Shell Crisis. In a letter dated 2 July 1916 Henry wrote: 'My diet is bully beef & biscuit, we cannot get bread'. In a fashion typical throughout history, it is the personal or familial network that stepped in when the bureaucratic one failed. In response to the food supply problems, Mabel wrote on 30 July 1916 that she sent Henry 'cakes. ... every week', a contribution typical of the support given from families up and down the country.

A project of his own: Henry's Baths

Henry was not a merely helpless actor at the Front, struggling to keep pace with the casualties and shelling. Naturally, there were moments, as Mabel calls them, of 'comparative rest' (16 May 1915) and it seems that in these moments Henry put his mind to helping the troops. Mud, lice and dirt seem inseparable from our understanding of trench conditions and were thought to have taken a serious toll on morale. The static arenas in which the conflict was fought meant that the conditions for comfort were so lacking that they became a hallmark of this style of warfare. On 29 August 1915 Mabel wrote that Henry himself 'had not been able to take his clothes off for 8 days & felt very dirty, as the mud was so thick that it splashed above his borrowed gum boots', saying 'it was a "very hot spot"'. The difficulty of the mud appears more than once in the diary, as an entry on 28 November 1915 shows, it was something worth writing home about:

'Henry says "the mud is something awful, it is ankle deep wherever you go
& a foot deep in some places"'.

It is due to this problem of mud and dirt that Henry started his project
of building a large bathing unit for the men. Mabel describes the project on
1 August 1915:

> Henry has been very busy behind the lines at Ypres, making great Baths
> for the men. They have proved a great success. He can bath 100 men
> per hour & hopes to extend it to 200 soon. Each man gets clean hot
> water & clean clothes. Henry has had to arrange the Laundry of 50
> women at a place 8 miles away.

The benefits this provided must have been gratefully received and immensely
comforting. Henry seems to have gone well beyond the RAMC's brief for

Figure 21: Henry (second from the right in the front row) with the other Officers (including
Basil Hughes D.S.O., author of *War Surgery From Firing Line To Base* 1918, first on the left
of the front row), taken in France circa 1916.

bath-house duties. Mabel wrote in the same entry that he 'has had to do nearly all the planning for the baths himself, as the engineers are all wanted in the trenches'. She goes on to explain how this is taking a strain, as he 'has asked for goggles (motor) & a scarf as he has sore eyes & a stiff neck from so much motor driving in getting & arranging things for the Baths'.

The baths became something of a large project with involvement from quite senior figures (it was probably around this time that figure 21 was taken, which shows Henry with Basil Hughes DSO who became an authority on war surgery). The diary records two separate occasions where Henry is making plans and having them approved, one on 27 September 1915: 'He is still much occupied with the Baths & had to go & see Lord Scarboro' & General Mends next door at the Territorial Headquarters about plans, etc. as they are going to send him out an asbestos building for the Baths for the winter'. Then on 28 November 1915 the diary recorded a visit from 3–6 November where he 'was on business in connection with the Baths & he spent much time with Lord Scarboro', who is the head of the Territorial Association & with Mr Brierly, the architect'. These entries indicate the length of the project, the resources given to it and the coordination Henry had with very senior figures.

Much progress had been made from the entry on 11 August 1915 where Henry seemed to be a one-man show 'very busy with his Baths' finding 'great difficulty in obtaining the necessary timber. He is building an ironing shed'. Due to its circumstances, not all that much is known about the baths project. Yet it seems clear that there was a desperate need for a large bath unit and that Henry responded to the problem by designing and developing a successful temporary building project to meet this need, under very difficult circumstances. Building on this, he later coordinated with senior figures to produce a more permanent fixture to be of use for the troops.

Medals

While the baths can be seen as one of Henry's major achievements, we know that he made other contributions, and that these came at a personal cost. While Henry was one of the lucky soldiers to come back, an entry on 20 July 1916 records that:

On the 13th I got a notice from the War Office that Henry had been slightly wounded. It said "Regret Capt. H. N. Goode was wounded slightly July 8th. Remains at Duty". He first wrote that a stone had struck him on the neck from the explosion of a shell, but "done no damage". By degrees it comes out that the stone knocked him down & he was dazed for some time & his elbow was injured.

This does not seem to be the only injury Henry received, as his obituary mentions that he was 'twice wounded and gassed'. We know that on one occasion the gassing was due to Henry choosing to remove his mask in order to operate effectively on a patient. Such was the effect of the mustard gas that six years after the war, in 1924, he lost the sight of his left eye and could no longer perform surgery. Having to remove his mask to operate effectively gives an idea of how very close to the front line some of these operations were performed. Even early on, Mabel was clearly worried about Henry, writing on 19 May 1915 that 'It is indeed a terrible war & it will be almost a miracle if he comes back unscathed'.

Yet Henry did come back and with the Military Cross (MC) and Bar (meaning his service merited him earning the Military Cross twice). In the army, the Military Cross was the third medal in order of precedence, only behind the renowned Victoria Cross and the Distinguished Service Order. He was awarded both MCs in short succession during 1918 (the year figure 22 was taken) and, as his obituary states, he 'was mentioned in Dispatches', meaning his name was specifically used in praise by superior officers in official reports to High Command. Given that Mabel finished the diary in 1916, we have no family record of the story behind the MCs but, as was common, a few lines explaining the reasoning for the award of the medals were published in the Gazettes of the time.

The initial granting of the MC was published in *The London Gazette* on 16 September 1918, and reads as follows:

Capt. (A./Maj.) Henry Norman Goode, R.A.M.C. For conspicuous gallantry and devotion to duty. He was in charge of the bearers collecting wounded, and frequently visited his posts under very heavy shell fire. He organised the evacuation of the casualties from the regimental aid

Figure 22: Henry, as an acting Major in 1918, the year he was awarded the MC and Bar.

posts to the advanced dressing station, frequently being obliged to alter his routes and establish new relay posts, owing to the heavy shelling. It was largely owing to his courage and energetic ability that the removal of the wounded was carried out in such a speedy and efficient manner.

At this time the war was becoming more dynamic and mobile. The Battle of Havrincourt, fought on 12 September 1918, was the first time the Hindenburg Line, the last of Germany's main defensive set of fortifications, was pierced. This was at the beginning of the 'Hundred Days Offensive', a series of Allied victories that essentially beat Germany out of France and ended the war. The baths prove that Henry showed initiative and he was also recognised by those around him as courageous and energetic when the Allies went on an all-out offensive against an increasingly desperate German army.

The second time the MC was bestowed (the Bar to the medal) was recorded in *The Edinburgh Gazette* on nearly the first anniversary of the Armistice, 11 December 1919, and reads as follows:

Capt. (A./Maj.) Henry Norman Goode, M.C, M.B., I/1st (W. Rid.) Fid. Amb., R.A.M.C.. T.F, From 29th October, 1918, till the morning of 3rd November, 1918, he was in command of the bearers clearing the divisional front. He was under enemy shell fire daily, and was buried by a shell on the 30th October. Throughout the whole time he worked, day and night with short intervals for rest, setting a fine example of fearless devotion to duty. (M.C. gazetted 16th September, 1918.)

Just weeks before the end of the war, Henry worked relentlessly to take soldiers back behind the lines to be operated on. As ever, enemy shell fire seems continuous and to have been buried by the force of an exploding shell gives a good idea of just how near Henry came to peril at the end of the war. Of all the praise in the two descriptions above the word 'fearless' used in the final sentence is the most poignant. To have been so devoted to his work, to save the lives of others in a field where his own was constantly at risk, and to have that rightly recognised is a great thing.

Figure 23: Stuart Goode, circa 1889, Kensington.

Stuart

Birth, Germany and the army

Stuart, the eldest of the children, was born in 1869. The diary suggests that Stuart benefited from his time in Heidelberg. An entry on 18 August 1914 calls him 'a First Class German Interpreter' indicating a good grasp of the language but there does not seem to be much evidence of other academic pursuits or interests coming from his schooling. It was Stuart who sparked the move back to England in 1887, as he wanted to join the British Army when he was 18.

The first official record of Stuart's progress in the Army comes from *The London Gazette*, (23 December 1890) which states that 'to complete establishment' he is to advance from Second Lieutenant to Lieutenant in the Bedfordshire Regiment, at the age of 21 (see figure 23 for a contemporary photograph). The next major commission was to Captain which was recorded in *The London Gazette* on 23 July 1898, when Stuart was 29. By this time, Stuart was very much the professional soldier, serving the British Empire at its apogee under Queen Victoria and spending time in India.

Stuart completed his Army service on 7 June 1910, retiring as a Major, as recorded in *The London Gazette*. At some point between then and 1914 he emigrated to Canada. Curiously, Mabel mentions on 29 August 1915 that Stuart had been '20 years in the army & only 3½ years on the Reserve in between', suggesting that he entered the Reserves in 1912 after a two year break.

In Canada, Stuart lived in a little place named Bonnington Falls, in the rural hinterland of British Columbia. Mabel wrote on 16 October 1914 that Stuart was busy 'growing his apples & playing tennis & helping to re-roof his little church' in what the diary indicates was comparative poverty, something of a quiet, simple and frugal life.

Into the fray and the trouble getting there

Like Mabel, Stuart seemed to see the war coming. Mabel recorded on the 18 August 1914 that 'Stuart has also written from British Columbia dated Aug. 2nd three days before the War was declared & he says that things look very warlike'. The passage goes on '& so he may see us sooner than he had expected', showing that Stuart was still very much part of the military. To come from Canada proved easier said than done, something which gave Mabel great anxiety.

Most of the early mentions of Stuart in the diary were reports about a lack of contact or difficulty in him getting to the Front. Initially, Mabel was convinced that Stuart would be among the first to help from Canada. The entry on 19 August 1914 stated: 'The paper says the Canadian Contingent will go direct into the Continent so we may not see Stuart after all'. This is followed by unease that Stuart has not made contact, with entries stating 'No more news yet from Stuart' (21 August 1914) and 'Stuart is still a mystery' (8 September 1914). Eventually, Mabel loses her patience and proactively tries to cajole Stuart into action by reminding him of his duty and how to go about re-entering service, detailing on 16 September 1914 how she:

> spent some time this morning in writing to Stuart & in finding the 'Times' of August 5th, which contains the Order from the War Office calling out all the 'Regular Reservists' & telling them not to wait for individual orders, but to present themselves forthwith & join their regiments. I cut off the sheet and sent it to him. How, after reading that Order he could still be waiting for his orders to proceed to England on Aug 14th & even now still puzzles me completely. I am sure no other Reservists did anything so feeble and silly. It is dreadfully trying & worries both me & Mother very much. We also wired to the War Office to ask if he had been ordered to come to England, and prepaid the answer but have had no answer. Neither have they answered Mother's letter of enquiry about him of last Friday.

This entry shows how much the family worried about Stuart not joining up early on in the war. At this time Mabel still assumed the war would be over quickly, making her sense of urgency perhaps understandable. The entry also gives a good impression of the social pressures that existed at the outset of the war. At this time, recruitment drives were starting to get into full swing and families became keen to show that their men were willing to fight. (Examples of the recruitment efforts and sentiments are illustrated in figures 4, 24 and 25.) The fear that Stuart was being 'feeble and silly',

Figure 24: 1915 recruitment poster. By this time both Henry and Stuart were abroad serving and Mabel was starting to feel the effects of the war. (*Royal Pavilion & Museums Brighton & Hove*)

and the worry this caused the family, reveals just how important it was to relatives that each household was seen to be contributing.

The delay is later explained as a result of Stuart wanting to get personal orders back to avoid paying for his own passage home. Mabel records on 21 September 1914 that Stuart:

> has written to Henry & is most anxious to come but wants an order so that he may not have to pay his own passage, which he cannot afford. Henry has written to Lord Kitchener about him, as retired officers are asked to do so, if they have not received their orders.

The lengths to which the family went to ensure Stuart could fight went right to the top – to Lord Kitchener himself, the man whose famous face adorns probably the most prominent poster of the time, literally embodying the call to sign up; a man synonymous with the war. The fact that this procedure seems to have been widely known about and recommended for people in Stuart's situation gives an impression of just how much uncertainty and confusion there was as the country mobilised for a large-scale war, along with a testament to the eagerness of households across the nation to have their men, like Stuart, enter service.

Eventually the family network stepped in to help Stuart join the mobilisation. After a reply from Lord Kitchener declined Stuart's services, Mabel wrote on 24 September that 'Mother has sent Stuart £50 to pay his passage home, if he thinks it is any use to come'. Mabel's comment is curious, as it alludes to the idea that Stuart's contribution was in

"Why aren't You in the Army?"

Figure 25: Postcard making light of the pressure for recruits. (*Tony Allen's WWI Postcard Collection*)

doubt or, more probably, that the war was supposedly near an end. It is made more interesting by a later comment in the same passage that the family think the reluctance for Stuart's services 'is economy on the part of the Government, as Henry says they … are evidently hard up'.

The eagerness to join up and get involved in the war is commonly remembered in scenes of queues at the recruiting office or recruitment rallies. Far less dramatic but as important were the efforts of family-members to encourage and support their men to fight – sometimes this pressure must have been immense. What the diary only hinted at is the reluctance that many men may have felt, as captured on Mabel's reflection on 16 October 1914 that Stuart 'does not seem keen'.

Over a century later, Stuart's motivation (or lack thereof) cannot be ascertained but if he was indeed disinclined to join, Mabel certainly felt a duty to change this and to chivvy him along to sign up. Unlike her attitude to Henry, whom she clearly adores, we can sense in the diary entries a certain asperity towards her elder brother – her exasperation at his 'feeble and silly' behaviour is one of the few passages in the diary where she comes close to open criticism of any family-member. The relief Mabel feels once she knows the family are playing their part is obvious in a short reflection on 7 January 1915: 'am really very glad they are both serving their country'. To get them both into the field was a concern of hers and she took it seriously.

The last war for an old soldier

Stuart left his quiet home in Canada for the battlefields of Europe on 19 November 1914. His war did not start well. Mabel wrote on 2 December 1914 that his 'interview in London at the War Office was disappointing. They did not give him any definite instructions'. This suggests either that Stuart was not much help to them or that there was some difficulty in the early war bureaucracy, or both. Exactly two weeks later, Stuart was appointed, as Mabel wrote, 'Deputy Assistant Adjutant & Quartermaster General to the 24th Division at Shoreham … worth £500 a year'. This was good news, as Mabel wrote on 18 March 1915 that 'the post is good & the pay excellent, an important point for Stuart'. One can sense the sisterly pride when Mabel sees her brother on 7 January 1915 finally in uniform: 'He came in all his staff grandeur of scarlet & gold cap & scarlet tabs on his tunic. The cap has a red band with a small gold worked lion surmounting a crown & gold oakleaves round the edge of the black eye shade'. It was not to last. Saying 'his next in command is too disagreeable & impossible to work with', by 18 March Mabel made it clear that Stuart had left that position and was looking for a new one.

It was not long before Stuart was to find the regimental posting that he went on to hold throughout his war service. Back with his old Bedfordshire Regiment, he took up a post on 11 April with the 4th Battalion. Mabel describes the role on 13 April: 'the 4th Batt. does the same work as the 3rd i.e. trains men & sends out drafts to the 1st & 2nd Batts. which are out fighting in France'. Stuart later gave an idea of his work, telling Mabel on 27 June that he is 'training young officers in 10 weeks or less'. The strain required to compel the army to train officers in that time is apparent in the diary's next sentence: 'Our losses each day are terrible, both officers & men. Generally between 100 & 200 officers every day in the Casualty List, & yet so little to show for it!'

Stuart's war work was a direct result of the need to train new officers to lead a burgeoning army and replace the heavy losses it faced. The role he played tells us much about the pressures of the war in 1915, just how difficult the situation had got for the Allies and how there seemed to be no end to the stalemate.

The death caused by the war is remembered by the poppies seen in every town and village, office and school across the country on Armistice Day; but war scarred and maimed as well as killed. The scale of the mutilation meant there was a drive to redeploy these men. A new Battalion was set up in July 1915 from officers and men unfit for direct combat to undertake police and guard duties. By 1 August 1915 Stuart had written that he had been reassigned, saying 'he & another officer have been ordered to organise regiments of soldiers who are too disabled for active service, to do garrison duty'. These duties did not mean that Stuart was far from the action. On 2 September 1915 Mabel wrote that Stuart 'is at Lemnos, in sight of the flashes of the guns in the Dardanelles at night'. Mabel clearly disapproves of Stuart's new work, saying: 'They were intended for India, but India refused to have them. It seems a poor thing that Stuart should be sent off for garrison duty with a number of physical incapables, after 20 years in the army & only 3½ years on the Reserve in between'. Her comments tell us a great deal about the attitudes prevalent at the time. She clearly does not see this work as worthy of Stuart's record and working with 'physical incapables' must have been a concept fairly unfamiliar to her. Despite her disapproval, for the rest of his war service, it was Stuart's job to help deploy those maimed but able to work which is telling of the war he was serving in.

As time marches on, the national memory of the war fades with each generation that passes, from this it can be forgotten just how visible the effects of the war were. Stuart's nephew, born in 1924, recalls how obvious the toll the war took was:

> As the son of a doctor I used to visit many houses because in those days it was normal for the doctor to visit his patients and as a child I would sometimes accompany him. It was common to see displayed photos of sons or husbands killed in the War. It was also common to see in the streets beggars wearing their medals.

For Stuart and Mabel in 1915, however, the reality of so many wounded and disabled combatants was new. The Government's decision to form a Battalion of those unfit for direct combat was one response to this reality, providing a role for Stuart from 1915 onwards.

Chapter 7

What we Have: Objects with a Story

The repeater watch

Henry's Great War repeater watch (see figure 26), made of gun metal, is a fairly dull and plain item in itself. Yet while barren in decoration, it is one of those items which have a story that illuminates an often forgotten angle on the war.

Figure 26: Henry's repeater watch.

Longstanding trench warfare was unprecedented, meaning there were new rules to staying alive, or rather, new things that invited death. Trench warfare on the Western Front was both static and dangerous: two sides, each backed up with artillery, dug into set defensive positions to stop the other making any progress, both trying to inflict damage on the other. In this new field snipers became an ever-present threat. Obviously, trenches were fixed and constrained locations; snipers could take position to watch the men go from one section to another and if a man were exposed then a shot could be taken.

Mabel alludes to this need to keep hidden and give off no identifying mark in an entry on 15 May 1915: 'they often have to stop on the way till things quiet down & can shew [sic] no light, not even a cigarette'. It is from this that the repeater watch becomes necessary, possibly even lifesaving. The beauty of the watch lies in the fact that it tells the time through striking (so the listener can hear the number of pings for hours and quarter of hours), meaning that Henry did not need to light a match to see the watch at night. Not needing to strike a light to tell the time meant Henry could avoid giving away his position to a sniper looking for a sign of life in the dark at which to aim. The watch was one of many items increasingly used in the trenches to adapt to the risks the new warfare posed.

The Ypres window panes

It was common for servicemen to bring back souvenirs from the war. Henry's youngest son remembers that 'after WW1 many houses in England boasted shiny brass cartridge cases (often referred to as 'shell cases')'. The war left behind lots of things by which to remember it. Of all the souvenirs from the war that the Goode family have, the Ypres window panes (see figure 27) have the most meaning.

Henry was stationed near Ypres, which suffered greatly from intense shelling over a sustained period. The beautiful stained-glass windows of the Cloth Hall (an impressive gothic building completed in 1304) were shattered when it was virtually levelled during the war (see figure 28 for a before and after). This destruction left pieces of the 700-year-old stained glass scattered all around. Running out through that half-desolated city, Henry occasionally collected glass in the short periods of uncertain respite from shelling. It was to be a scene all too familiar with the decimation witnessed in the thirty-one years between 1914 and 1945: soldiers and civilians doing their best to salvage what they could of Europe's heritage.

Henry took these fragments of glass back to England. His son recalls that in the 'early 30s Rosetta, Henry's wife, bought a kit with lead strips for making stained glass windows and assembling the pieces of Ypres glass into a window pane. She achieved a successful pattern and then had it made up professionally'. From this, one large and one small pane were made and act as reminders of what little remains of the structures blown up by the Great War.

Figure 27: The Ypres window pane, with glass from the Cloth Hall.

Figure 28: The famous Cloth Hall in Ypres (built in the 13th century and completed in 1304) before and after the war, showing the scale of the war's destruction. It is from here that Henry got the stained glass for the Ypres window pane.

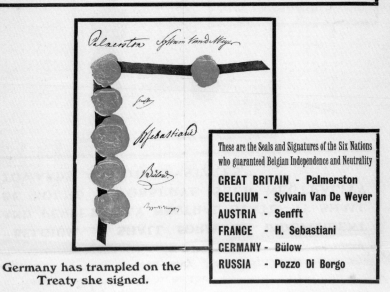

Figure 29: Poster from 1914, galvanising support for the war by justifying Britain's entry into it. (*Royal Pavilion & Museums Brighton & Hove*)

Chapter 8

Mabel Goode's Diary of the Great War: 1914

August 11th 1914

'What a time! Never has there been anything so tremendous in the History of Europe before, and it has all come about within the last 10 days, certainly as far as England is concerned.

A week ago last Saturday,[1] Henry & I were enjoying ourselves at the Archbishop's Garden Party at Bishopthorpe & there was only a sufficient darkening of the horizon with war clouds to form a main topic of conversation & make things interesting. Now, 10 days later War has been declared between England, France & Russia and Germany, the long-expected war, come suddenly, as long-expected things generally do and 2,000,000 soldiers are facing each other with great determination for 300 miles along the dividing frontier of France & Germany.

York is full of soldiers, all the larger spaces & buildings are being used as barracks, while many of the Schools, including the Training College in Lord Mayor's Walk & the Bootham Quaker School are being converted into Hospitals by the St John's ambulance association. Everyone is anxious to help in some way, for instance my Mother has given 2 beds for a hospital & I have been collecting money & things necessary for it along St Leonards, Blake Street & Davygate.

The railways have been taken over by the government on account of the necessary moving of Troops, but they are causing as little inconvenience as possible to the people.

I will give an account of our family experience, which is typical of thousands of others during the last 10 days. On Sunday morning, Aug. 2nd, the day after the Garden Party at Bishopthorpe, my brother Henry was to go to his Training Camp (Territorial) at Scarborough for a fortnight as he had joined the R. A. M. C. T. 9th Brigade West Riding Field Ambulance in the Spring. He was very busy going round to pay last visits to his patients, so

Nancy & I finished his packing for him & Imeson took him & his baggage to the station in the car to catch the 11.35 train to Scarborough, where he was to join the rest of this Brigade from Leeds.

On Monday war was declared between [blank][2] & we heard that all the Territorials were ordered to return to their Headquarters. We expected to hear from Henry, but heard nothing. The Navy was mobilised. On Tuesday, at luncheon time he appeared & said he could stay the night but must go into Leeds in the evening for further orders. He said he had scarcely any sleep since leaving us & had been up entraining all the night before. That afternoon we were all in a state of great excitement & tension, as the order for the Mobilization of the army was expected any moment. Germany had violated her Treaties & invaded Belgium & England had sent her an Ultimatum to retire from Belgium & respect her neutrality (as France had at once promised to do). Germany was to send a reply by midnight that Tuesday. After luncheon Henry went into town to get a strong pair of brown boots to wear with his Khaki & I had to go out to tea. On coming back I found Henry outside Mr Campbell's door, talking to him & Mr Nelson with much animation. On seeing me, Mr Campbell pointed to the Union Jack, which had been hoisted over the Territorial Headquarters next door to us & said that meant that mobilisation had been ordered. He was already in his chaplain's uniform, as he is Chaplain to the Royal Garrison Artillery here (Territorial). So the die was cast! And all hope that England might be able to remain neutral was at an end.

When Henry returned from Leeds at 10.30 pm, his first words were "Well, it's good-bye to mufti"[3] & he said he had to be at Leeds by 9.30 the next morning for parade. We persuaded my Mother to go to bed, but he & I set to work & repacked all his kit, so that he had only his Khaki & its belongings with him. He also took his camp furniture & bedding valise.[4] It had been decided that he should stay with his Captain Dr. Stewart in Leeds, who had very kindly offered to put him up. We had finished the packing about 12.30 both very tired, poor Henry having had no real rest since Sunday. We had to get up soon after six on Wednesday morning, so that he might have breakfast & catch his train. Mr Shann (the Locum) & I both went to see him off. We met Mr Harry Scott at the Booking Office going to fetch his company from Selby. He is Captain in the 5th Yorks. And Mr Hassle, in his khaki, got into Henry's carriage. He managed to get home for a few hours on Sunday, &

on Monday was suddenly ordered to Selby with a detachment and Captain Lister.

It has been a time of wild rumours of battles & encounters of the Fleets in the North Sea. But the great & splendid fact is that unexpected resistance made by the Belgians at Liége, which has checked the Germans & given the French time to mobilise & the Russians to get ready on their side.

Servia [sic] also has so far beaten Austria back.

Thursday, August 13th

This morning just before coming down to breakfast, I heard the telephone in Dr Shann's room, above mine. I had heard him go down just before, so knew there was no one else to answer it. I went up & found it was Henry. He had rung me up late yesterday evening from Selby to ask if I cared to come over & see him this morning. Of course I jumped at the idea, especially as I wanted to take a photo of him in full uniform. So this morning he rang up to ask me to bring him a pint mug, white enamelled & get his initials put on. When I told Dr Shann just before breakfast, he promptly left his breakfast & went off to buy one. He also bought a camp knife & fork, as a present for Henry. I was to get to Selby between 10 & 11am as the rest of the Brigade was to arrive about then. I cycled into town first & got some leather boot laces Henry had asked for & some enamel to paint the initials on with, as it would have been impossible to get them dry in time. I also took a tin of cocoa for him. Imeson took me to the station in the car to catch the 10.30am train. I was lucky at Selby in falling in with a nice little girl, who was going past the High School, as I did not know the way & it was about 1 mile. The little girl said there were 4 or 5,000 troops in Selby. We saw a good many odd ones about.

The High School stands back from the road, with some magnificent trees in front. A sentry guarded the gate, but let me go in, when I told him who I wanted to see. There were some soldiers outside raking the ground smooth & the one in charge undertook to find my brother & asked me to wait in the office. Henry came in a little while & took me over the building, which was very well suited to the purpose. The ward I saw had low beds on wooden trestles & the room where the men sleep had a bare floor. Henry said the men slept on the floor. He & Captain Lister sleep side by side in a small room in their valises! – i.e. a waterproof sheet & a thin mattress under them.

I took 3 photos on the lawn in front of the house, with the 2 flags, the Red Cross & the Union Jack as a background. Then Dr Stoddart arrived & as the officers wanted to confab together, Henry had to leave me in their little room, where they slept, I stayed there quite an hour, I think, before my brother could come back. He said he had been seeing sick & had to go out to a Fever Isolation Hospital 2½ miles away. He would have liked to wait & see the rest of the Brigade arrive, they were expected to come that morning. But he had to go & we went nearly as far as the Abbey together. We saw nothing of the arriving Brigade.

I bought a paper at the station as it announced on the placards that war had been declared between England and Austria & I found it was true. The 2 great armies, French & German, have only met at outlying points so far.

Figures 30–31: Henry in the photos Mabel described in her 13 August 1914 entry.

Figure 32: Photo taken by Mabel in York Station of men struggling to entrain the big 'gray' horse, as mentioned at the end of her entry on 13 August 1914.

At the York station I saw the troops entraining some horses. One big gray [sic] one was too tall. He bumped his head & refused to go in, in spite of coaxing with hay. Finally, a coat was thrown over his head & about 10 soldiers pushed & pulled each side & one beat him & they got him in by main force.

August 14th

There is no news of any great importance about the war, but the Germans seem to be pushing their way through Belgium by sheer force of numbers & in spite of terrible losses. They have not captured the forts at Liége but have made a detour & are 20 or 30 miles from Brussels, pushing, it is supposed towards Antwerp.

Nothing seems known of any English Expeditionary Force. An English Correspondent from Brussels writes that they are asking all round there "Where are the English?" Mr Campbell, our next door neighbour & Chaplain to the Territorial Royal Garrison Artillery, says they left today for Hull, to embark there. They volunteered to go abroad.

I spent some time this afternoon making a top for a camp stool I have promised for the St John's Ambulance Hospital here.

There seems no great danger of a famine at present, as our trade routes from Canada and America are being well protected by Cruisers & there are only 5 German Cruisers trying to intercept the vessels.

On our East coast no lights are allowed at night in windows facing the sea & they are digging trenches along the coast, certainly at Hull.

August 15th 1914 Saturday

There is no very exciting news from the Continent, but what there is confirms the fact that both Germany and Austria are being defeated by the Allies, where ever they have met. The great attack has not yet begun.

Things are quieting down rapidly. Prices are very little higher, except for a few things like eggs & butter.

Most of the troops who were in York have moved outside, the Seaforth Highlanders to Strensall[5] & the Irish Fusiliers to the Knavesmire.

Boats are even allowed to fish in the North sea within certain areas. Nothing is heard of the German or English fleets except the Cruisers who are attacking & protecting our trade respectively across the Atlantic.

Our next door neighbour, Mr Campbell, Chaplain to the Territorials (Major) has just been in to shew [sic] us his new Khaki uniform, which is de rigueur now, even for Chaplains. He says the R.G. Artillery are not actually embarking yet but have gone to Hull by road.

The papers have been recommending everyone who has a little ground to use it for planting vegetables in, as they may be wanted later on. It seems rather farfetched, as we grow most of our fresh vegetables in England, I should think, but we are going to plant a few in a corner of the garden, where the grass is poor & should be dug up anyhow.

August 17th

The great battle has not yet begun, but all the news so far is good. The Germans & Austrians are being drawn back on all sides in the small encounters.

The Kaiser has gone from Berlin to Maintz [sic], in order to be nearer to the scene of operation, but it seems improbable, as far as one can judge, that he will prove himself a second Napoleon.

He is very much annoyed with Italy for insisting on remaining neutral. In fact on all sides, his little deep laid plans have mis-carried. He undoubtedly expected that Italy would join Austria & Germany & that England would be obliged to remain neutral on account of the Irish Home Rule trouble. It is certainly splendid & surprising even to ourselves, the way in which all internal differences have been completely put aside & the Irish, instead of flying at each other's throats, are prepared to fight side by side for Old England & most excellent troops they will make too.

It is a great thing to feel that our cause is a just one & one may surely believe that God has helped us, for things are wonderfully in our favour. Only Germany & Austria are against us, while on our side are France, Russia & Belgium & the Japanese Navy. Italy is neutral & all our colonies are supporting the Mother Country nobly. Canada has sent us a million bags of flour & ½ million bushels of oats besides promises of men & ships & America is warmly in favour of our cause. It is the cause of progress, peace & civilisation against militarism & despotism. The only other likely ally of Germany & Austria is Turkey, but I should not think she would be of much account, as her government is so corrupt. There has been a splendid response to the Prince of Wales' War Relief Fund, £1,200,000, in 10 days. One wonders a little, will it really be all wanted & all the hospitals that are prepared all over the country.

August 18th

The great news today is that the English Expeditionary Force has landed in France. The fact & all movements in connection with it have been most carefully concealed from the public & kept out of the press, but we are now allowed to know that the troops embarked at Southampton & landed at Boulogne, everything working without any hitch or a single casualty. We are not told how many, only that General Sir John French who is in Command went on to Paris & visited the President, rejoining the Army later.

There is a rumour that the German Crown Prince is wounded & being nursed at Aix.[6]

With regard to ourselves, Henry has written to ask for dictionaries of French and German, as he has to examine his men in French & German. His own knowledge of them will be useful to him now. He also tells us that he is only allowed to be away for one hour, so we cannot hope to see him at present. My eldest brother Stuart has also written from British Columbia dated Aug. 2nd three days before the War was declared & he says that things look very warlike & so he may see us sooner than he had expected, as he is a Reservist Major & a First Class German Interpreter,[7] he ought to be of some use to his country now.

Several editions of the 'Press' have been published every day at short intervals ever since the war began & I generally buy 2 during the day, sometimes 3, they only cost ½ d. Today the 'Evening Press' was being sold in the streets at 12am!

August 19th

There is not much fresh news about the war, but it is reported that there is a general forward movement of the German army, which is massed along a front of 115 miles in Belgium & Luxembourg & it is said that the Kaiser has given personal orders to his generals about it. It is expected that the Germans will occupy Brussels before long & it is not to be defended. It is not considered that it will be of much value to the Germans, except that

Figure 35: Photo taken by Mabel of Strensall Camp, 1914.

Stuart is still a mystery. He wrote to his lawyer at Leeds on Aug. 14th to say he expected to get his orders almost immediately & to land at Liverpool.

Recruits are coming in very well. Yesterday was a record recruiting day in London, 4,833 men being enrolled.

September 9th Wednesday

The news is very hopeful today. There is a tremendous battle raging in France, to the East of Paris & down the border of Alsace & Lorraine. The Allies have taken the offensive & in spite of desperate efforts of the Germans, they are being forced back towards the frontier & away from Paris. The British captured a battalion of infantry & some guns.

The Censor has allowed the mention of the arrival of the 250,000 Russians to pass, so we may presume that it is really true.

The Indian Contingent of 70,000 have certainly started & possibly arrived at the front & the 1st Canadian Contingent has arrived in England. There are 300,000 men involved in the stupendous struggle in France.

It is reported that Germany has brought or is bringing up 2,000,000 more men to reinforce her Eastern border & help the Austrians against the Russians.

September 12th Saturday

The last 2 days have brought excellent news from the Front. The German army for some unknown reason swerved aside from Paris, when within quite a short distance, about 20 miles. This gave the Allies a chance which they at once seized. They took the offensive, the British on the left (North) in the post of honour & attacking most fiercely, drove the enemy back ten miles, forcing their left wing towards the Northwest in a semicircle. Yesterday came the grand news that the 10 miles had become 40, both the British & French armies pursuing the Germans, capturing many prisoners & guns. In the placards the Germans retreat is described as a rout.

The Belgians, gallant little folk, have also rallied & assumed the offensive & recaptured several of their towns from the Germans. The Austrians are still being crumpled up by the Russians & are of no account. So that one really does not see how the War can go on very much longer. The French say it will be over by Christmas. It seems quite likely.

Henry, who was here yesterday, speaks of it lasting a year, but I think the wish is father to the thought, as it seems his Brigade are quite likely to go to the front & he is anxious for the war to last, or rather, to get out before the war ends.

Our Locum (Mr Shann) left us today & Henry has arranged that Dr Micklethwait shall do the work for him. He thinks it will keep the patients better together & cost less.

Still no news of our elder warrior. Mother has written to the War Office to ask if they can give us information about him. Personally I quite expect him to turn up any time, quite unconscious that he should have written to tell us what he was doing.

The streets are full of soldiers, many of the young ones in red tunics, instead of khaki. The government has run out of khaki cloth & has ordered 100,000 blue serge uniforms from Leeds for recruits, which will be changed to khaki, if they are ordered aboard. Russia has also ordered 100,000 uniforms from Leeds.

The papers still do not say if the rumoured Russians & the Colonials & Indians are fighting at the front. There are a number of German prisoners in Exhibition Buildings, as the Castle jail is full.

September 15th Tuesday

The German Retreat still continues & they are reported to be in a miserable plight, short of ammunition & food. They contested the passage of the Aisne most stubbornly, 16 times did they make a bridge across it & each time the French destroyed it with their guns.

This great battle, lasting more than 10 days, is described as the Battle of the Marne.[17] Both the German & French Generals issued a general order, which spoke of the coming battle, as the most decisive one for their nation. 3,000,000 men were engaged in it. The Germans tried time after time to make a fresh stand, but the Allies pressed forward fiercely, forced them from each position in turn & pursued them relentlessly. The enemy have abandoned numbers of guns, ammunition wagons, baggage and all kinds of stores in their flight. The French sunk a large number of barges of German ammunition, which may account for the fact that they were obliged to cease their rifle fire in the midst of the fighting. The German prisoners admitted that they had had no food for 2 days.

The Belgian Army has done its share most gallantly & has engaged a large force of Germans who would otherwise have been able to reinforce the sorely pressed North Eastern German army.

When finally overpowered by numbers, the Belgians retired behind the forts of Antwerp.

The Crown Prince has had to remove his headquarters from Namur & his army may yet be surrounded & cut up.

September 16th Wednesday

I spent some time this morning in writing to Stuart & in finding the "Times" of August 5th, which contains the Order from the War Office calling out all the 'Regular Reservists' & telling them not to wait for individual orders, but to present themselves forthwith & join their regiments. I cut off the sheet and sent it to him. How, after reading that Order he could still be waiting for his orders to proceed to England on Aug 14th & even now still puzzles me completely. I am sure no other Reservists did anything so feeble and silly. It is dreadfully trying & worries both me & Mother very much. We also wired to the War Office to ask if he had been ordered to come to England, and prepaid the answer but have had no answer. Neither have they answered Mother's letter of enquiry about him of last Friday.

Henry is still at Strensall, under canvas. He comes in to tea every 2nd or 3rd day in the car, which we send in for him. He can ring us up on the telephone from Strensall Golf Club. He always brings 1 or more of the other officers with him & it makes things quite cheerful. His Brigade are expected to move on somewhere else this week.

The war situation has not changed much, except that the Germans appear to be making a fresh stand. They are said to be in a good position in the North East of France & we shall probably hear of another big battle being in progress shortly. We are promising to take in 2 Belgian ladies. It is rather an undertaking for Mother, but we both feel we must do what we can for the poor things. Their nations' bravery has probably saved England from invasion & devastation by the brutal Germans.

September 21st Monday

There is a great battle in progress, the Battle of the Aisne, which is a river North of the Marne. The Germans are strongly entrenched & are making a very stubborn stand & have made furious onslaughts both on the French & the British, but all have been splendidly repulsed in spite of heavy losses & the Allies have slightly gained ground. The furious artillery duel goes on day & night. At night the search lights of the Germans constantly pass over our lines & reveal our positions. I don't understand why we do not also use searchlights, but apparently we do not. All accounts of the battle so far speak of the great pertinacity of the English (almost inhuman courage, our correspondent calls it) & the admirable dash of the French & say that the Allies are most cheerful & quite confident of victory. At the same time the Germans are admitted to be making a fine resistance, but they are still throwing away their men recklessly by attacking in close waves, which the Allies mow down in a terrible fashion.

As if Lorraine were not a sufficiently horrible crime, the wicked Germans have bombarded & burnt down Rheims Cathedral. It is sad beyond all words. One of the very most beautiful of Gothic cathedrals of the best period. A thing which can never be replaced. And what do they gain by it? Inside the Cathedral were many of their own abandoned wounded & the Red Cross was flying from it. Many of the unfortunate German wounded were wounded anew by their barbarous comrades. They really behave more like madmen than a civilised nation. In 1870 they spared Rheims & also in the war before that. Now they spare nothing, neither women, children, old men or sacred edifices.

We have received a reply to our wire about Stuart, it runs "Not yet ordered home" Military Secretary. So they probably grudge the money for his passage. It is certainly a considerable item, £25 to £30. He has written to Henry & is most anxious to come but wants an order so that he may not have to pay his own passage, which he cannot afford. Henry has written to Lord Kitchener about him, as retired officers are asked to do so, if they have not received their orders.

September 24th Thursday

Henry received a reply from Lord Kitchener in the form of a printed paper declining Stuart's services for the present. He signed the envelope in the corner "Kitchener". So Mother has sent Stuart £50 to pay his passage home, if he thinks it is any use to come. We think it is economy on the part of the Government, as Henry says they are cutting down their bacon allowance in the mornings & are evidently hard up.

As regards Henry it is settled that his Field Ambulance is to go out to the Front in November or December. One will be very anxious, so many of the R.A.M.C. men are killed, wounded or taken prisoner. There is a Captain Seatehand R.A.M.C reported killed in today's List. We knew his brother Dr Seatehand in London, when he was at Henry's Hospital & he lives near Tadcaster now.

There has been a British Naval disaster, 3 cruisers, the Aboukir, Cressy & Hogue have been sunk by German submarines in the North Sea. About 1,000 men were saved out of more than 2,000; chiefly by a Dutch vessel. The crews all behaved splendidly & there was no panic or disorder.

The great Battle of the Aisne is still going on, neither side gaining any great advantage, in spite of furious fighting & many bayonet charges, which the Germans, contrary to their usual practice, have not always fled from, but sometimes returned with equal fury.

The French say the great encounter is only now beginning. The front extends over 100 miles.

The Allies are gradually getting round the enemy's right flank, which may threaten the German communications. Three English airmen dropped 3 bombs at Dusseldorf on a Zeppelin shed & set it on fire.

A German cruiser "Emden" fired 9 shots at Madras & set 2 oil tanks on fire.

Henry told us tonight that the reason of the extraordinary hasty retirement of the French before the Germans was the result of treachery on the part of the 2 French generals. Kitchener realized that something serious must be wrong, went over to France & arrested the 2 generals, who had made feeble excuses for not supporting the British & had ordered the retirement. He found one had a German wife & the other had retained important despatches unopened. So both were at once shot. Presumably they had been heavily bribed.

The Belgian King's chauffeur was carrying him towards the German lines, at a review, when the King noticed it. As he refused to stop, the King shot him with a revolver & on him was found a paper from the Germans offering him 1,000,000 francs for doing it.

October 4th Sunday

And still, though I write after an interval of 10 days, the Great Battle of the Aisne is going on. Still the 2 great armies face each other from their entrenchments & now one & now the other gains some slight advantage. But on the Allies' left wing the fighting has been most fierce, where the British are, especially, & the enemy's right is being more & more forced up to the North, in spite of reinforcements on their side & most furious onslaughts. Their efforts to "wipe out French's contemptible little army" have been not only in vain but always repulsed with heavy German losses.

The enemy are bombarding Antwerp with their heavy guns, but so far all the forts are said to be intact.

The more one reads of the cruelty & atrocities of the Germans in Belgium the more are they proved to be not only true, but more horrible than they were originally reported. Their treatment of the women & girls has been brutal & cruel beyond all words. The unarmed men are shot, often as a sport. The houses are set on fire & the Germans amuse themselves with shooting at the wretched inhabitants when they are fleeing from them.

The German Emperor goes about in a train composed of ten carriages, painted dark with a red cross on the roofs. He has his staff with him & a body guard of 10,000 Prussians & a large number of detectives from all parts of Germany. And his movements are kept very secret, the old coward! The Crown Prince does at any rate go with his army. He appears to be at least personally brave.

The dropping of the bombs on the Zeppelin shed at Cologne caused quite a panic among the inhabitants & they have fixed up airship shooting guns on roofs to be ready for next time.

We have not seen much of Henry lately, until yesterday. He has been busy at his hospital & also has a bad cold.

Yesterday he was coming into York, bringing Col. Sharpe to the station in his car & Col. Sharpe said to him "You have a very bad cold, you had better stay at home for the night". So Henry did so. He brought, of course, nothing with him, but Evans & I found him all he wanted, except a toothbrush! And he had a hot bath & a hot bottle in his bed & seemed better this morning. He came to the Minster with me & we walked afterwards by the river with "Rags". There was plenty of time, as it was an Ordination Service & we left after the first part. Then we had a hare for dinner, a very favourite dish with both of us & just before 2pm he had to leave in the car & fetch Col. Sharpe from the station. My Mother is not well & is in bed at present.

Mr Campbell has got his appointment as military chaplain, after all, but not with his own garrison Artillery. He is appointed one of the 2 chaplains for the 2nd West Riding Brigade & is now at Riby [Riby Park] near Grimsby. He went on Tuesday.

October 10th Saturday

Yesterday Antwerp was bombarded by 200 German big siege guns & part of the city was in flames. The Governor refused to surrender the city & warned the inhabitants before the bombardment began. The poor folk had to flee as best they could & a quarter of a million refugees are now in Holland. 30,000 Antwerp refugees arrived in a town of 10,000 inhabitants in Holland. Every house was packed so full, it could hold no more! The garrison defended bravely, but their guns were too small to resist or overcome the great German howitzers & apparently they have had to leave the city & cross the Scheldt.

The King & Queen were some of the last to leave. The Government has been transferred to Ostend & there is a possibility that it may have to be moved to London.

The 12 o'clock placards announced the entrance of the Germans into Antwerp. I bought a paper & found it was unofficial news, but it is so probable that one may fairly well believe it.

The English have had the German ships in the harbours, about 30 & 20 others destroyed, burnt.

London has been warned by the authorities not to show any lights except those necessary to direct the traffic. In spite of the warning some of the large shops have meanly tried to attract customers by keeping their lights on as usual.

There is no doubt that the Germans intend attacking England & London in particular with their Zeppelins. They are reported to say that it will be at the end of October when they have Antwerp & the coast of Belgium for a base. Perhaps if they wait too long, their intended base may be in the hands of the Allies, as they are pressing the Germans back somewhat in the North & have almost pushed them out of that part of France.

The great Battle of the Aisne still goes on, without much change in the South. Rheims, alas! has been bombarded several times. Even in today's paper it is reported to be again being shelled. There is a picture in the "Daily Mirror" today of a hospital containing wounded which was shelled by the Germans & it shows what a wreck they made of it & says they wounded again the unfortunate wounded lying in it. There was no time to remove them & they had to lie there with the shells bursting over them.

No news from Stuart at all. Henry is still in Camp at Strensall. It is cold at night & he has had several times to break the ice for his morning tub, when getting up at 5.30. They have all been given bottom boards for their tents.

October 12th Monday

The fall of Antwerp is indeed a sad blow. The garrison appealed to our Navy for help & they lent them 3,000 men & big guns to help them. But it was in vain & when the town was obliged to surrender the Belgian Army & their artillery left by train for Ostend, but 20,000 or 25,000 did not get away in time & they were driven across the Dutch frontier & so forced to lay down their arms & are interned. Sad to say one of our Naval Brigades, 2,000 strong, also shared the same fate. The other Naval Brigade & the guns got safely away. There are said to have been 60,000 Germans before Antwerp.

Of course, the Germans are wild with joy at the surrender of the town, though it seems doubtful whether it will be of much practical use to them.

Henry & Col. Sharpe & Capt. Stewart were here to tea today & they think there must have been treachery in connection with the surrender of the forts & also in connection with the Belgian & English troops getting forced into Holland.

Several German aeroplanes have dropped bombs over Paris, killed 4 & injured 17 people & injured Notre Dame. Our Gravesend people have issued a warning to the English people that in case a Zeppelin comes over they should take refuge in the lower rooms or in the cellars.

October 16th Friday

Henry came home on Wednesday with a bad throat, which at the camp was thought possible diphtheria, but, thank God, it has not turned out to be quite so bad as that. It is a septic throat from overworking, after the weakening process of inoculation for typhoid.

Col. Sharpe was fetched from the station in our car at 9.30 this morning & came in to see Henry en route for Strensall. He said he must stay quiet several more days & only be up for a few hours this afternoon, so he got up for tea. He had engaged to vaccinate the Hon. Edward Wood[18] for smallpox at 5.30, so he had to get up anyhow. Mr Wood is to go out with his yeomanry, the Yorkshire Dragoons some time, but they do not know when. H. says he is about 7 foot high. I did not see him.

Ostend appears to be the next immediate objective of the Germans & their big guns. It has been evacuated & is now a deserted city.

York has accommodated 50 wounded Belgian soldiers, 30 in the County Hospital & 20 in the Convent. The Lord Mayor appealed for funds & Mother & I sent him something as soon as possible. The 1st Canadian Contingent has arrived at Plymouth amid great enthusiasm on both sides. The great British and Canadian Liners took all day arriving.

We, or rather, Mother, had a letter from Stuart the same evening, (yesterday) & one half hoped he might have written it just before coming over with the Canadian Expeditionary Force, but it was not so. He is still at Bonnington Falls,[19] growing his apples & playing tennis & helping to re-roof his little church. He has written to the War Office (a fortnight before writing to Mother) & says he may possibly come over with the 2nd Canadian contingent, if he is still there. We at home do not think he will, as he does not seem keen, like the Canadians are.

The possibility of a German invasion is discussed yesterday in the "Times". It says they would sacrifice all their ships & 50,000 men to take or destroy London.

Henry is employing his enforced rest in considering how to place an Ambulance body on his Daimler chassis & take it with him to France, or will it be Germany by then?

October 23rd Friday

The Germans took possession of Ostend, but it seems unlikely that they will be able to retain possession of it long, as several of our battleships have got within range & have been bombarding it with the big naval guns. Three monitors[20] which were being built for Brazil & which our Government took over at the beginning of the war have been especially useful, as they are able to go close inshore. The firing between Ostend & Nieuport has been incessant on both sides. The Germans have brought up some of their big guns to reply to our Fleet, but they have some difficulty in getting the range. One of our shells burst in the midst of a German General & his Staff & killed them all.

Altogether the Allies are holding their own splendidly & it seems almost certain that there will be a general retreat of the enemy before long. They have failed to pierce the Allies' line at any point & their trenches are in a terrible condition. Typhoid & Diarrhea are rife amongst their troops & from the diaries found on the Germans officers' bodies, it is evident that they are getting very disheartened & depressed.

The French, on the other hand, are in good spirits & have half a million fresh troops ready to be thrown forward wherever they are required.

The gallant little Belgian army has been resisting the Germans bravely & keeps up its spirits in spite of the sad plight of their country. They tell the Germans that they are coming back before long & then there will be a little bill to pay.

On the Eastern frontier the Russians are driving the Germans back in a hurried retreat from Warsaw. They allowed the Germans to come almost up to the city, keeping their forces out of sight, & then fell on them in overwhelming strength & hurled them back & they are still retreating, much demoralized.

So things are looking cheerful for the Allies all round.

One of our Submarines A.3 is much overdue & it is feared that she has gone down, perhaps struck a mine.

Several of the German cruisers are active in capturing our steamers, notably the "Emden" & "Carlsuke".[21] There is a list of 13 steamers which the latter has sunk in this evening's Post.

Henry's throat is much better. He has been sleeping at home until this evening. But he will only have this one night under canvas, as they all move into York tomorrow. Fortunately it is mild & dry tonight. The Field Ambulance are billetted in Nunthorpe Hall, near Knavesmire.

October 25th Sunday

The great battle on the Belgian coast is still in progress, the first in history in which there has been fighting on land, on sea & in the air all at the same time.

On the coast the Allies are holding their own & the big Naval guns are causing awful losses among the Germans, 15,000 are reported to have been buried in one field alone & many have had to fight standing up to their waists in water in the trenches.

Henry moved into York (Nunthorpe Hall) yesterday with his Field Ambulance. He & Capt. Stewart (who was yesterday gazetted a Major) came in to supper & we all drank the latter's health in port.

Seventy two cruisers, etc. are hunting the Emden, Karlsruhe, etc.

October 28th Wednesday

The battle on the Belgian coast is still raging & becoming fiercer than ever. Both sides are fighting with the greatest determination. It is said that the Kaiser has commanded that Calais must be taken at all costs. The German losses are terrible. Our big naval guns mowed the men down in masses wherever there was an opening among the dunes where they were taking cover from the Allies' land forces. They have now brought up guns & placed them along the coast & claim that they have driven our ships away.

There are a good many Belgian wounded soldiers in York & 300 Refugees have been taken in, in families, in the country around.

Henry & Capt or rather Major Stewart came last night to tea at 7pm & went with me to a Lecture on Belgium given by Dr Sarolea[22] in the Festival Concert Rooms. He had been 5 weeks in Belgium as War Correspondent. He gave a very sad picture of it & said the Germans had done more damage in 2 months than all the European countries have done in Belgium in 500 years. He also said that the whole Belgian people who are left in the country have only 3 or 4 days of provisions & will then literally starve. Poor things! It is terrible & one sees no remedy, nor could he suggest one, except that the Americans might help. The room was crowded & many were standing & they had to have an overflow meeting afterwards.

There are about 10,000 troops in York now & all the public buildings & empty houses are full of them.

November 1st Sunday

The War has been going on for nearly 3 months now, & seems likely to be longer than ever. There have been several complications since I wrote last. Portugal has joined the Allies & Turkey has thrown in her lot with Germany, led away by her lies & misrepresentations. This will mean trouble in Egypt, if not in India. In South Africa there is a Revolution, first it was Colonel Maritz & a not very large force, but since then General De Wet & General Beyers have headed a rebellion in the north of the Transvaal. General Botha has remained strongly on the side of the British & was so rapid in his movements that he took Gen Beyers completely by surprise at Rustenburg & defeated him. The majority of the Boers are said to be quite loyal & very indignant at the rebellion. Of course all these things will lengthen the war.

There was a terrible wreck yesterday morning a mile South of Whitby. The Rohilla, a British India Steam Liner, fitted up by the Government as a Hospital Ship, ran onto the rocks in a terrible storm. She was on her way from Queensferry to Dunkirk to fetch French wounded & was unable to see her way owing to the storm & the darkness & the absence of any lights along the coast. The Whitby lifeboat went out to her twice in spite of the tremendous sea & saved 60 of the 180 people on board. Then the lifeboat was damaged on the rocks & could not go any more. The vessel broke in two & when we last heard there were still many survivors on the wreck. The Scarborough lifeboat came in answer to urgent appeals but could not get to the wreck. She was brought by a tug. The vessel is only ¼ mile from shore & 30 men saved themselves by swimming, but several were drowned.

The German cruiser Emden has again distinguished herself. She rigged up a 4" dummy funnel & flew the Japanese flags & approached close to a Russian cruiser & torpedoed her so that she sank. She sank also a French submarine.

November 9th Monday

Several important things have happened since my last entry. Turkey has joined Germany & has tried to stir up the Moslems in Egypt & India. England & the Allies generally have declared war on her & so far she has been beaten in the encounters that have taken place between her & Russia. Her attempt to stir up the Moslems in India has resulted in a wave of loyal enthusiasm for the Emperor King. In Egypt things are quite calm & martial law has been declared.

Russia is gradually rolling her millions towards Breslau & Berlin. The Germans are retreating before them, as the Austrians did & have had terribly heavy losses of men & guns & ammunition.

The Battle of Ypres for the possession of Calais has been most fierce & bloody. Mrs Beutley's youngest son Cyril, was killed in it. A nice young fellow, only 20, in the Manchester Regt. But the Allies have more than held their own, in spite of the presence of the Kaiser with his troops. Many of them (the Germans) are only lads, 15 to 17. Large numbers have been taken prisoner or have surrendered without fighting.

Several German cruisers came almost as far as Lowestoft & fired at the guardship [blank space, presumably to be filled in later],[23] they did not do much damage & made off in haste as soon as some more of our battleships went to her assistance, but they threw out mines & sank one of our submarines which was following them. Naturally the raid caused some alarm & much excitement in England. Henry's Brigade were ordered to hold themselves in readiness in case they were wanted. One saw the troops going about the streets in full kit, greatcoats etc. & the officers with their swords on & field glasses. Henry telephoned up to ask us to make some brassards, i.e., white armbands with the red cross on for the officers, so I bought the material & we all set to work. I cut them out, Evans stitched them in her machine, Mother sewed the buttons on & Nancy made the button holes & by 10pm we had got our 10 complete.

However things quieted down & the Brigade is still here.

But they have received notice from the War Office that they are next on the List for foreign service in France, so they may go any time.

Yesterday they had a Brigade Service in the Minster at 9.15am & the Archbishop preached a splendid sermon. I went, as Henry's sister (no public were admitted). It was most impressive. There was no choir, we had 3 fine hymns & the sound of the mens' voices was grand, like a deep roll of thunder. I watched them march past, leaving the Minster. They stepped out with good spirit, but many struck me as of poor physique & evidently Leeds city-bred lads. I have had my first poem printed 'To the R.A.M.C.' in the Yorkshire Herald of Oct 31st. Certainly war inspires poetry. Nearly every day there is some poem in the Times & in the Yorkshire Herald.

November 15th Sunday

One of the chief events of the past week has been the capture or rather burning of the Emden, the German raiding cruiser which has done £3,000,000 of damage to the Allies shipping. The "Sydney" an Australian Cruiser, found her & sank & fired her with a few shots & hardly any casualties of her own. About 300 of her crew of 320 perished, but Captain Von Müller & the Hohenzollern Prinz[24] were saved & allowed to keep their swords.

Today comes the news that Lord Roberts[25] died at 8pm last night. It is sad. He was 82 & went across to France to see the Indian Contingent, caught cold & died of pneumonia. I am sorry he is gone. There is no one left like him. If only the English would have taken his advice about National Service, how it would have shortened or prevented this war.

In the North there is terribly fierce fighting, but the Germans make no progress. The carnage is terrible & such large numbers of prisoners. Yesterday we had 13,000 Germans & they captured 800 of our men. The Russians are pushing steadily on towards Silisia & East Prussia.

November 22nd Sunday

On Friday my Mother heard from Stuart that he was coming home in the C.P.R. boat Messanabee,[26] 12,000 tons, carrying only 2nd & 3rd Class passengers. He wrote from Nelson on Nov. 5th.

Today she has had another letter which explains, written at Bonnington Falls on Nov. 3rd. He has been ordered by the War Office to return home & report himself as soon as possible. He was to leave Montreal on Nov. 19th, so he should arrive this week.

There has been some severe weather which has caused a partial lull in the fighting in France, though they say our men are fairly comfortable in the trenches.

Henry went past with his whole Brigade a few days ago on a route march. He says they are getting really fit to go & Col. Sharpe says even the Leeds Rifles are ready to face the Germans now.[27]

130 of our wounded arrived in York yesterday, some of them had been fighting in the trenches 2 days before, so quickly had they been brought.

November 27th Friday

Yesterday came the sad news that the battleship "Bulwark" had suddenly blown up & that 700 or 800 men who were on board were killed. She was a battleship of 15,000 tons. The cause of the explosion is unknown. It is surmised that either her powder had deteriorated or that a shell fell into it. In any case her powder magazine blew up. There was a loud roar, a sheet of flame & a dense volume of greenish smoke & what had been a splendid battleship lying peacefully at anchor with the band playing on board, was a mass of twisted iron & debris & a death trap for 700 men. I do not know of anyone on board, but most of the men came from Portsmouth.

The more cheering news is the success of the Russian armies in Poland. They have cut the German army in two near Lodz & it is expected that they will inflict a crushing defeat on it.

No news yet from Stuart. He should have arrived at Liverpool by now.

A German invasion is much talked of & trenches & wire entanglements are I believe made all along the East coast. I should like to see them. Our ironclads have bombarded Zeebrugge, which the Germans were making into a naval base to use against England. The harbour & works for putting together 6 submarines were destroyed. But the town was not shelled.

Our Airmen also have distinguished themselves. They have flown, 6 of them, to Friedrichshafen, the place on the Lake of Constance where the chief Zeppelin works are, & dropped many bombs, they say, destroyed a nearly completed Zeppelin in its shed. One man, Briggs, was wounded & forced to come down & was taken prisoner. It was 125 miles each way over German territory.

November 30th Monday
Two momentous events have taken place today in our home circle. In the first place we were getting rather anxious about Stuart, as we heard nothing of him on the Missanabie. And this morning at 9.30 Mother got a wire from him from Liverpool, saying he was going up to London today & hoped to be in York tomorrow evening.

The 2nd event is that Imeson has joined the Army Service Corps as Motor Ambulance Driver. He is to leave us tomorrow & go to Doncaster to join them. He was away all day. Henry had told him what to do & Henry was here at dinner time & Imeson came back & we had him in & he told us all about it. Henry promised to get Col. Sharpe to write or telephone to have Imeson as driver for one of their 7 Ambulance Motors. He & Henry have tucked up the car[28] or whatever is necessary for its long rest. How long? I wonder.

Mother has already marked a dozen khaki pocket handkerchiefs for him & I have promised him the khaki muffler I have knitted. I am sorry he is going but very glad he has joined, as he had scarcely anything to do & was going to seed.

December 2nd Wednesday
Stuart got home yesterday evening at 9.50. Henry, who was here to dinner, went to the station to meet him & brought him here. He looks very well, but has something wrong with his right arm, which makes it painful when he uses it in certain ways & very weak. Henry & he think it is from playing tennis & that some muscles are torn. His interview in London at the War Office was disappointing. They did not give him any definite instructions. So he is awaiting them here & in the meanwhile does not know what kit he will require, whether for home or abroad.

The fighting in Belgium has been less fierce, probably because the Germans have had to move more troops to the Eastern side to oppose the masses of Russians, or they may be preparing for a fresh attack on Calais.

There has been a dreadful explosion at a Lyddite factory near Leeds & several people killed in it. One suspects German spies.

December 10th Thursday

Stuart is still at home & still has received no orders from the War Office. He & I went over to Scarborough yesterday for a halfday trip. I wanted to see the defences. We found a barricade of sandbags across the main street going down to the sea, about 3/4 of the way down, with loop holes to fire through. Stuart said 4½ feet was the correct height for the loop holes & for trenches. At the bottom of the same street a fairly wide barbed wire entanglement had been constructed, quite as high as a man's height. There were several other sandbag & barbed wire defences defending the entrances to all the main streets up to the town. The trenches were rather disappointing. They seemed very few & far between, but we found several small (short) ones made in some of the asphalt paths, dug out of them to the required depth & the sides boarded up. There were some in front of the Grand Hotel & we were told there were more round the North Bay, but did not see those.

The Great War goes well for the Allies. In South Africa the rebellion has been crushed out, General DeWet is a prisoner & General Beyers was wounded while crossing the Vaal River & drowned & the body has not so far been found. General Botha has acted with great vigour & promptness. Now he is preparing to invade German West Africa. In the Pacific a squadron of our battleships has attacked 5 German cruisers & sunk 3, the Scharnhorst, Gneisenau and Leipzig. The other 2, the Dresden & Nurnberg are being pursued by our ships.[29]

The Servians are again defeating the Austrians.

The Kaiser is in Berlin & very ill with pneumonia & nervous breakdown. He is said to behave with great violence to those around him.

I have heard from Mrs Jencken[30] that my R.A.M.C. poem was so much liked by a lady to whom it was shewn by one of Mrs Jencken's friends that she asked permission to recite it & did so at a Red Cross Concert where it met with much applause. It is delightful to think it has been of some use! Mrs Jencken has sent me her Valse.[31] I am afraid it may not be a great success as people are not thinking of valses this winter & there will, I suppose, be very few balls.

December 16th Wednesday

Just a week since Stuart & I went to Scarboro' & today, at 8 am the town was shelled by the Germans, 4 German cruisers, it is reported. The telephone & telegraph wires were cut. The news came out in a special edition of the Yorkshire Press about 11. The inhabitants fled & are still fleeing to York & Leeds, many of them in their night attire.

Miss Barry has just been in & says she saw a Belgian refugee lady in Brown's Drug Stores who had just come from Scarboro' & had her house shelled & was in a state of collapse from nervousness & terror.

Hartlepool is also officially reported shelled & Whitby unofficially. They say a great battle is raging in the North Sea.

Of course many people must have been killed & injured, but very little definite is known about that at present.

It seems there was a mist over the sea which enabled the ships to get so close in. The lady described the noise of the bursting shells as "a hundred thunderstorms rolled into one". I have always said they would come in a fog.

Stuart got a wire on Saturday, saying he had been appointed Deputy Assistant Adjutant & Quartermaster General to the 24th Division at Shoreham. It is part of the 3rd New Army & his General is Sir John Ramsay, a retired Indian Army man. Stuart left us on Monday for town & meant to go on to Shoreham on Tuesday. It is a staff appointment &, Mr Campbell tells us, worth £500 a year.

At lunchtime a number of troops went past, presumably on their way to the station, singing cheerfully. Miss Barry says they were the 6th West Yorks. We have not heard that Henry is moving.

December 27th Sunday

Hartlepool was so badly shelled by the German cruisers that more than 100 were killed, including a good many soldiers & of course many more were wounded.

Whitby was less severely handled, but 3 or 4 people were killed & the Abbey was a good deal damaged by the shells.

About 20 people were killed in Scarboro' & many injured. I went over to see it the day after the bombardment. Several of the hotels & many private houses along the sea front had all their windows broken & many great gaping holes in them. The low, one-storied restaurant in front of the Grand Hotel was a wreck, every great pane of glass gone & a mass of debris & fallen masonry in the centre, where some people were looking for fragments of shells. One shell had struck the ground below a house & broken the strong iron railing into small pieces, smashed all the windows & bent & twisted the balcony 2 stories above. The train returning was crammed, largely with Scarboro' people fleeing, in case of another bombardment, they said a despatch rider has come in to say that the Germans would be back in 2 hours. We were 15 & a parrot in a large cage in our carriage.

We heard today that Ned Berry is in the trenches with the Ghurkhas.

December 28th Monday

This Christmas time has been a great time for the flight, not of angels' wings, but of the wings of aeroplanes of all kinds. Two days before Christmas the first German aeroplane to fly over British soil dropped a bomb on Dover near the Castle. Fortunately it fell harmlessly in a garden & only made a hole.

On Christmas Eve a German aeroplane was seen flying high over Sheerness. It was fired at by our anti-aircraft guns and fled East, dropping nothing. On Christmas Day the English Navy made an attack on Cuxhaven with sea planes carried by destroyers & light cruisers. Two Zeppelins came out against the 7 sea planes, but were driven off by our aircraft guns on the ships & our sea planes dropped a number of bombs. All the flyers were brought back in safely except one.

So the vaunted Zeppelins do not seem very formidable after all & the submarines were evaded by our ships. All our troops in the trenches & elsewhere had plum pudding served out to them by the government, apart from private gifts & many of the men are said to have had 5 or 6 plum puddings apiece altogether.

The Government are proposing to compensate for the damage done to Scarborough, Whitby & Hartlepool by the German bombardment.

Henry came in this evening, before going on to dine at the Residence & meet there his Brigadier General Macfarlane, & he said he had been to a lecture, in which they were told that, at the present rate of progress, the war might last 10 years! Let us hope the rate of progress may increase!

Henry came to us for Christmas Day dinner & afternoon & evening.

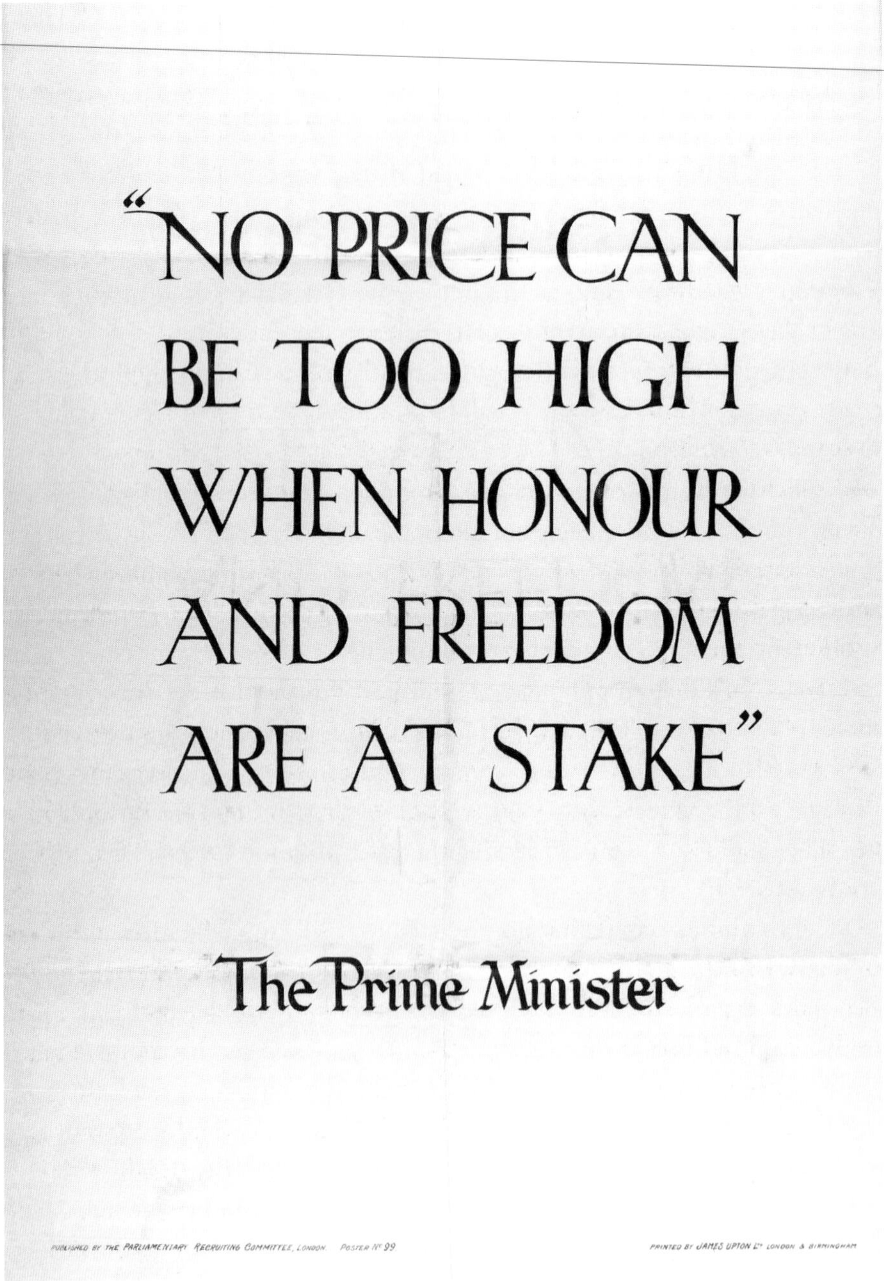

Figure 36: Recruitment poster from 1915, illustrating the graver tone used to convey the scale of the struggle with the Central Powers and what was at risk. (*Royal Pavilion & Museums Brighton & Hove*)

Chapter 9

Mabel Goode's Diary of the Great War: 1915

January 7th Thursday

On Friday we got a card from Stuart to say he was coming that evening or Saturday morning. A wire rather later said "arriving 10.15 tonight". So we made ready for him. He came in all his staff grandeur of scarlet & gold cap & scarlet tabs on his tunic. The cap has a red band with a small gold worked lion surmounting a crown & gold oakleaves round the edge of the black eye shade.

He stayed till Tuesday morning. We got him to have his photo taken to make a pair with Henry's, so I hope to have a good pair of photos of my brothers in their war costumes, just head and shoulders.

It was a pity that Mother was so poorly with bronchitis while Stuart was here but his visit did her good & fortunately Henry's London lectures which he was to have gone up for on Saturday were postponed, so he saw a good deal of Stuart. On Sunday they walked together to Skelton[32] & took Rags as Henry had to see Peter Hill. Stuart took Henry's bike and black rubber boots back with him.

Henry & I both saw him off at the station. I took a 2½d ticket, as no one is allowed on the platform without a ticket. He was to spend Tuesday at the Haywards & go on on Wednesday to the Hayes-Sadlers & back to Shoreham on Friday. I felt very proud when I was with my 2 warrior brothers! And am really very glad they are both helping their country. Henry's latest is that they have been definitely told that they go abroad in the middle of March. We have lost another of our battleships, a pre-dreadnought, the "Formidable". About 600 of the crew were lost out of 890. It was either a mine or a torpedo, no one seems to know which & it happened in the Channel. The Russians have defeated the Turks at Ardahan[33] in the Caucasus & the French are pushing forward somewhat in Alsace, so that the Allies are getting on by degrees. But of course the weather is against any severe fighting.

Figures 37–38: Stuart (left) and Henry (right) in the photos Mabel described in the entry on 7 January 1915.

Stuart told us the Indian troops could not stand the wet in the trenches & have been placed further back, out of the firing line. So Ned is safe for the present, I hope. I sent him some chocolate from Mother & me.

Three Zeppelins, accompanied by aeroplanes, were seen over Calais & Dunkirk yesterday, but did not drop any bombs.

January 9th Saturday

It has been admitted by the Government that the "Formidable" was sunk by 2 torpedoes from a German submarine.

The French are making some progress in Alsace.

Henry has at last induced Col. Sharpe to apply for his promotion to a captaincy.

There were 2 articles in yesterday's "Times" regarding the shortage of doctors & recommending that the ones left should be as much safeguarded as possible & those at the front not allowed in the trenches.

Henry met Mr Gedge today & he told him he was going out as a chaplain to the troops & asked him to inoculate him.

January 21st Thursday – Whitby
It is a long interval since I wrote last in here but the bad weather has prevented any very extensive operations either in the East or West. Except for a severe defeat of the Turks in the Caucasus near Erzeroum, by the Russians, there is no striking event to record abroad. The Russians are slowly & steadily pushing forward towards East Prussia & Galicia & Austria. The Germans are sending a large force with a nucleus of 80,000 German troops against Servia.

In the West the French have pushed forward somewhat in Alsace & the Germans have had some successes near Soissons, where, it is believed, the Kaiser is commanding in person.

Two nights ago, at 8pm. several aerial visitors from Germany, supposed to have been 2 Zeppelins & 1 aeroplane passed over Yarmouth, Cromer & Sheringham & dropped bombs. They did a good deal of damage, chiefly to private houses & churches & succeeded in killing 4 people, 2 women, 1 soldier & 1 youth of 17.

The weather favoured them, being misty & the places chosen for attack were, as usual, undefended ones, the raiders escaped uninjured. But it shews how little real danger is to be feared from them. The air raid has caused great indignation in America. The Americans can see what the Germans appear unable to, the difference between dropping bombs on airship sheds & arsenals & military stores, as the Allies' airmen do, & dropping them on harmless people, including women & children & private property. There are great rejoicings in Germany at the cowardly attack by their pet Zeppelins.

I am staying here for a week & went this afternoon to see the bombarded houses near the station. They seem to have aimed at the latter & struck quite a number of houses, chiefly smallish ones, near it. Most of the windows & holes are boarded up & the glaziers are very busy on several houses. Some have already had their brickwork repaired.

February 14th Sunday
Ever since I last wrote the weather has been wet & cold, with only an occasional fine day & this has affected the War, especially in the West. The trenches have been half full of water & the mud has been so dreadful

that officers, writing to the Times, say that everything they had on & even their hands are thickly plastered with it. Many of our men get their feet frostbitten with the ice cold water they have to stand in. So that, although there is fighting every day & a daily list of casualties, no large numbers of troops have been sent out.

Last Friday the English made a great aerial attack on the German ports in Belgium, 34 Naval seaplanes & aeroplanes taking part in it. They attacked Ostend, & other Northern ports & destroyed a railway station & did other damage. The object was to prevent the Germans from using the places as bases for attack against England by water or air. All the pilots got back safely, though Graham White fell into the sea & was picked up by a French vessel.

On the East side there has been some very fierce fighting. The Germans are said to have lost very heavily, the Russians have had to retire from East Prussia.

Henry came today, with Lieut. Hughes in time to go to the Minster service at 4pm. He brought news that their brigade has received orders to move in 10 days time to Lough in Lincolnshire. The Ambulance have not yet received their orders, which puzzles them a good deal.

Prices are going up. Flour is 48/a sack or 50/ & coal is 35/ – 39/ a ton instead of 15/ – 19/ a ton.[34]

But there is no scarcity of food, as there is in Germany, where the Government have taken over the food supplies & only allow ½ lb of flour per head a day. They issue bread tickets. But it is rather cutting their own throats, as now the Allies can seize all vessels carrying foodstuffs to Germany, as being for the Government & therefore for military purposes, whereas before private German firms could not be prevented from having food brought them.

Mr Hughes takes a serious view of the probable length of the War & says that Germany is getting supplies of food & copper through the neutral countries; Holland, Italy & Sweden. He also says there are 8,000,000 German Americans in America & that they influence the President against the Allies.

February 18th Thursday

I must write a few lines today, as this day begins the German submarine attacks against English food supplies. They have threatened to torpedo all our merchant vessels & also neutral ones, which are bringing us supplies.

The traders & shipping people are taking it quite calmly & insurance rates have not gone up. But rewards are offered for any vessels which sink or ram or give warning about submarines of the enemy. There has been another successful aerial Raid by the Allies on the Belgian ports.

The Germans in Eastern Prussia have driven back the Russians & invaded Russia.

Yesterday the first batch of exchanged prisoners arrived in England, 3 officers & 105 men. They say they were fairly well treated in the hospitals, but very badly fed otherwise. They had food which in England would be given to the pigs & not even enough of that & if they complained, they were told that "you are starving us". They are undoubtedly short of food supplies. All these poor fellows are badly damaged, as only those are exchanged, who can take no further part in the war.

February 19th Friday

The first day of the pirate blockade passed off without, so far as we have heard, any of our vessels being sunk or torpedoed. Although somewhere off America the "Karlsruhe"[35] (cruiser) has sunk 4 or 5 merchant vessels of ours.

All over England we are more or less expecting Zeppelins. Though they have lost one or two lately. One fell in Sweden & was burnt up. Its motors failed to act. They seem to be hopeless failures!

At all street corners are hung up placards shewing the different shapes of Germans & English airships & aeroplanes. I have bought one also & hung it up outside the drawing room. People have been warned in the papers to seek refuge in their cellars or the nearest house, if they are out of doors. We propose going into our basement. But I think York is as safe a place as any.

February 27th Saturday

Today there is the announcement in the "Gazette" that Henry has been made a Captain.

I was sitting in the dining room after breakfast, reading the "Times", when, to my surprise I heard Henry letting himself in with his latchkey. He came to tell us of his promotion. I had not seen it. Really neither Mother nor I expected he would get it, as the rule is 3½ years as Lieut. before being promoted & even during this war they seem to have kept to the rule & indeed very few R.A.M.C. Captains have been made in any Field Ambulances. He is delighted & so are we. General Kenny helped him about it, as Major Clyde & Col – sent the papers back & would not recommend him.

Imeson, on the other hand, has been discharged & has come home today. He has taken a place as chauffeur to Dr Jackman of Kirby Moorside at 28/– a week, so he is doing well financially. There seems to have been much mismanagement about the motor drivers, who objected to the long useless drills & marches & not being sent abroad.

Several of our ships have been torpedoed, but nearly all the crews have been able to get away. But the armoured merchant cruiser "Clan MacNaughton" has been mined or torpedoed & all officers & men on board drowned.

The wind has been too high for any Zeppelins to come over but a few days ago a hostile aeroplane flew over Colchester & dropped a few bombs there & in the neighbourhood.

I hear from Col & Mrs Jencken that they heard the explosion, but thought it was a gun giving some signal & they went peacefully to bed & sleep, while the aeroplane probably passed over their garden.

March 18th Thursday

I have been lazy about writing up my Diary lately, but one good reason has been that I have had to spend every available evening in making out Henry's bills for him. He can come so seldom that I have pressed Evans into service & she has helped me several evenings. Then when Henry comes, he only has to send them out. Yesterday Evans left us to go home to her mother who has had Influenza & also misses her husband very much. He died only 2 or 3 months ago & Mrs Evans is 83, rather old to live quite alone. But Evans is to come back to us as soon as she can.

With regard to the War 2 chief events have taken place. First, the Allies attacked the Dardanelles by sea. We have used our largest battleship, Queen Elizabeth, & her great guns have destroyed the forts at the entrance & also some of those further inside also. Of course many other English & also French ships have assisted. There have been few casualties except on the "Amethyst" which was shelled from some of the inner forts when reconnoitring. So that it is expected that within a reasonable time & with more favourable weather, the Allies will be in Constantinople & the Black Sea will be opened up to Russia.

Figure 39: A photo by Mabel of the 'new splendid horse ambulances' mentioned in the entry on 18 March 1915.

The second great event is that the British have begun their great forward move against the Germans in the West. They took the Germans thoroughly by surprise in the Battle of Neuve Chapelle & gained a mile of ground covering 3 lines of trenches. The Germans lost 17 to 18,000 men in casualties. Ours also have been heavy but so far only the officers' names have been published, 200 in 3 days' Lists of Honour.

Henry has hopes of going aboard in April, especially as they have been given 3 new splendid horse ambulances with rubber tyres.

Stuart is, I am very sorry to say, giving up his post on the Staff, as D.A.A. & L.Q.G. at Shoreham, with the 24th Division. He says his next in command is too disagreeable & impossible to work with & he has sent in an application to return to his old Bedfordshire Battalion. The man who had his post before him evidently found the same difficulty. Such a pity, as the post is good & the pay excellent, an important point for Stuart.

March 31st Wednesday
Stuart has been relieved from his staff appointment, his successor being an Artillery man from the Front, who had passed the Staff College. Stuart has applied to join his old Bedfordshire Regt., but is at present free & has gone

to Shrewsbury to join Henry there, who is taking his first leave, 4 days, since the War broke out.

Przemysl has fallen, a great blow to the enemy, as it is the key to Cracow & means that Galicia is finally lost to the Austrians. The German submarines have torpedoed a good many of our vessels. As a rule most of the crews have been allowed a few minutes to save themselves, but yesterday a submarine torpedoed the liner "Falaba" before the passengers & crew had time to get into their boats & the German brutes jeered at the poor struggling creatures drowning in the ice-cold water, about 112 drowned. Such is German Kultur!

April 4th Sunday (Easter Day)
Stuart & Henry came home yesterday evening. They did not arrive until 9pm, as the 7pm train had been taken off. Trains cannot be depended on now. All the Easter excursion trains have been cancelled this year, owing to military requirements. Stuart has not yet heard what he is to do from the War Office.

Henry was present at a service for the troops at the Minster at 9am this morning. I saw him after it, among a group of officers outside, while the men streamed out of the West door, & I spoke to him. He told me that they had been told definitely that they are to go to France on April 18th. He is pleased, though he would have liked best to go to the Dardanelles. It has been a happy Easter Day, as Stuart came with me to the Early Service at 8am & Henry & he & I all went to the 4pm Minster service & heard "I know that my Redeemer Liveth" & the Alleluia [sic] Chorus beautifully rendered.

There is no very important news about the war. The cruisers both of the enemy & especially of the Allies have been active, but they do not appear to do very much damage. The German submarines torpedo one or two of our ships & also neutral ones every day, but they in return have had some of their submarines rammed & sunk.

The Russians are said to be forcing the enemy back & getting over the Carpathians.

The Archbishop preached today first to the troops in the Nave & then to us in the Choir at the 10.30 service.

April 13th Tuesday
Henry is really gone and to France! It seems difficult to realise that one will never now find his cap & coat hanging up in the hall or flung down

Figure 40: A photo by Mabel of Henry with Rags, no longer sent 'half wild with delight' after Henry left, as mentioned in the entry on 13 April 1915.

Figures 41–42: (Above and below) Henry marching his troops to the front, as referenced in Mabel's 13 April 1915 entry.

in the dining room, when one comes in; that no longer will he come in to tea, bringing us his latest news & sending Rags half wild with delight. And yet I ought to realize it, since I got up at 5am this morning in order to see him pass on his way to the station from Nunthorpe Hall. I was roused by Nancy's alarm, borrowed for the occasion & set out at six with Rags & the camera, as it was a beautiful fine morning. There was no sign of any troops about the station, so I walked on & presently heard some troops singing & saw them coming towards me from the Mount. It turned out to be Henry's section, with him marching at the head of them. They stopped to wait for the ambulance & I was able to speak to Henry & take 2 photos of the men & of him with them. I followed them to the station; taking some more photos of the waggons, etc., saw Col. Sharpe & Lieut. Hughes & caught Henry for a quiet little goodbye outside the station & came home about 7am. Later I met Mr Campbell & his sister. He also had been at the station (at 5am.) & saw and talked with Henry.

Yesterday Henry managed to come in to tea & an early dinner at 7pm & said goodbye to Mother & took various last parcels with him. He had to leave early as reveille was at 4am this morning. Major Stewart came in yesterday morning to say goodbye to us. Mother saw him & I just missed him, to my regret.

Stuart also has left us. He went on Saturday. He has been attached to the 4th Battalion Bedfordshire Regt. & is stationed at Dovercourt, which is quite close to Harwich & Felixstowe. Mother heard from him this morning that the 4th Batt. does the same work as the 3rd i.e. trains men & sends out drafts to the 1st & 2nd Batts. which are out fighting in France. He also writes of seeing torpedoes & destroyers & that Winston Churchill was round there on Sunday.

The Russians are pushing on the Carpathians & the Austrians, helped by the Germans, are making a desperate effort to outflank them, as otherwise they will lose Hungary.

Not only the Ambulance, but also the whole of the 3rd Brigade, which were here, have left York today for Harrow. The whole Division (West Riding) consisting of the 1st, 2nd & 3rd Brigades, some Irish Horse, Artillery, etc. are all going out there. So York will soon be empty of troops. But today large numbers also arrived, of Reserve Batts., which are going to be in camp at Strensall.

April 16th Friday

On Wednesday we had our first Zeppelin alarm. Mother & I were just having our cocoa nibs at 9.30pm, when there came a weird, penetrating sound, & just as we were agreeing that it was the syren [sic], the doorbell went. We found it was a young couple asking for shelter. He was in khaki, in the Army Pay Dept. & she explained that she had been through the bombardment at Scarboro' & it had made her nervous. We all went down to the basement, the young couple were put in the pantry & Mother & I into the kitchen. The maids brought us down some comfortable chairs & we settled down to wait [for] developments. The syren sounded again & we concluded the Zeppelin must be coming nearer. Presently the 2 young people, after he had helped to turn off the gas at the meter for us, made up their minds to go home, as it was not far away.

I rang up the Dunnington-Jeffersons on the telephone & found they had not heard anything of the syren, as I expected. We had good fun getting ourselves comfortable in the kitchen, using Nancy's bicycle lamp & my little electric torch to fetch down chairs, duvets & wraps. I wondered a little that we heard no explosions. Looking out into the street I saw the dark forms of the people shewing against the subdued light of the doorway of the theatre opposite, as they streamed out. The street (as indeed the whole town) was completely dark, so much so, that a man lighting his cigarette made a bright light amid the darkness. All the trams stopped running & everything seemed strangely quiet. About 11.30 Mother suggested that she should go to bed & as her bedroom is on the drawing room floor I thought she might. I went to bed in the drawing room, Evans in the Consulting room couch & Price & Nancy in the kitchen, the latter on the table! I did not sleep & having heard the trams running again I got up at 2am & went to bed, first going into the kitchen to tell the maids that they could go also. We came down rather late the next morning & it was somewhat disappointing to find from the papers that there had only been one Zeppelin & it passed over Blyth & Southwards, within 6 miles of the Elswick Works & out to sea again, never being within, I suppose, 80 miles of York. Not of course, disappointing that it had not come nearer, but that we had had our night disturbed without real necessity.

Last night 2 or more Zeppelins passed over Lowestoft & Harwich about midnight. Neither of the raids have done any great damage, nor has one person been killed, so far as we know at present.

No news yet from Henry.

April 27th Tuesday

We have had several letters from Henry. He had a pleasant crossing with meals given by the Lifeboat Fund, to which they all subscribed. It seems to me a misuse of money given for a certain object. They slept the night at their landing place (Havre?) & were cold in a shed. Next day they entrained, went a long round by train, spent the next night in the train & detrained the next morning. Of course he does not tell us where he is, but evidently in France, as he mentions graves of French soldiers round about & a frog pond in the garden of the house they have made into a temporary hospital.

Besides Neuve Chapelle, the British have had another successful fight & captured Hill 60, south of Ypres, after mining & bombarding it. The Bedfordshires took part in the assault after being for days in the trenches below it. Our casualties were not very heavy & the German counter attacks were all repulsed. The machine guns mowed them down as they came up in masses. The Germans have gained some ground & several villages North of Ypres & forced back the French by using asphyxiating gasses, blown by the wind towards the French trenches. And the Canadians on the French right were exposed & had to retire in conformity with the French & had heavy casualties. But later they regained the guns they had to leave behind & took back a village & behaved splendidly altogether.

The brutal Germans are ill-treating the unfortunate British prisoners, tormenting them & half starving them & in some camps they all suffer from itch & dysentery. Their clothes are taken away from them.

I have got some jute to make sand bags, as the papers say the troops need them by the million.

The 3rd Brigade which left here with H's Ambulance are in the trenches & the Dean mentioned it last Sunday & asked people to pray for them. The poor old man quite broke down. A large force has been landed near the Dardanelles by the Allies.

May 7th Friday

The effects of the asphyxiating gas used by the Germans near Ypres is too horrible. Those who do not die at once, suffer from slow, increasing suffocation, lasting sometimes one or 2 days. This is because the gas causes a foamy liquid in the lungs which increases & gradually fills all the lungs & then the mouth & then you die. It is the most horrible form of scientific torture. And those who do not die from the suffocation, always suffer from acute pneumonia. What fiends they are! They say half the soldiers who came into hospital suffering from the gas only, quite unwounded, have died.

By employing this diabolical method of attack the Germans have gained several villages round Ypres & moved their line a little more West, but thanks to the splendid bravery of the Canadians they did not break through the line. The Canadian losses have been very heavy.

The Germans have retaken some of the trenches on Hill 60 by means of employing asphyxiating gases & we are still fighting to turn them out.

In the Dardanelles there has been fierce fighting & the Allies have defeated the Turks & won a good foothold in the Gallipoli Peninsula.

When Henry last wrote, he was going into the trenches that same day. He asked for some tinned things, tongue & sardines & milk & a homemade cake to be sent to him. Mother has sent him 2 kinds of respirators to save him from the effects of possible poisonous gases. I hope we shall hear again soon. We heard last on Tuesday.

Last Sunday evening Miss Barry came in to say that Mrs Dunnington-Jefferson had heard on Saturday evening that Wilfred, her youngest son, had been killed in action.[36] It is very sad for them. Fortunately the elder son, Jack, is on the Staff in the Intelligence Dept. & so less likely to be killed. Wilfred was only 23.

This evening the papers announce that the Lusitania has been torpedoed with 1900 passengers & crew on board, near Liverpool. It is not known whether the crew or passengers escaped. They received a S.O.S message in Liverpool & many boats went out to help her, but we know no more at present.

Two days ago the Germans shelled Dunkirk, with great shells fired, it was at first thought from ships, as their line was 20 miles from Dunkirk, but it was found to the Allies' amazement that the Germans had actually 1 or

2 big guns which carry 20 miles. They were silenced by our airmen. It is a startling discovery. They are a more formidable foe than I expected.

May 16th Sunday

The torpedoing of the Lusitania has raised a storm of indignation in the United States & among all neutral nations. About 1500 lives were lost, among them many Americans & Canadians & a large number of young children & women. She was apparently struck only by one torpedo & sank in 18 minutes. There was more panic amongst the crew than among the passengers & one passenger said that if there had been no panic 500 or 1000 more lives could have been saved.

This cold-blooded murder of civilians at sea & the use of the poisonous gases have quite altered the feeling of our troops towards the Germans. Before there was a good-natured dislike & tolerance, but now there is a bitter hatred & a demand for reprisals. The Times correspondent suggests that we should use gases which cause temporary unconsciousness, without poisoning or cruel after effects & that seems to me a splendid idea.

We had 2 intensely interesting letters from Henry this morning. He had organised a hospital which he & Lieut. Hughes ran between them & Henry said in previous letters that he had twice running been up till 2am. attending to the wounded coming in. Then things became rather quieter & he got a comparative rest. In my letter today, written on the 12th, he says that last Sunday they had a "big scrap" there & they had to take off their coats & roll up their sleeves & work for all they were worth & that the state of many of the wounded was pitiable & the injuries terrible.

Since then things have been quieter again & he has handed over the Hospital to "Stewey" & he & "Hughy" are living in an ambulance in a village which is shelled every day. They visit the aid-posts from there every morning & evening, with bullets whizzing & sputtering about them. He says "it is very exciting!" And they often have to stop on the way till things quiet down & can shew no light, not even a cigarette. So he has got his wish at last & is quite "at the front". It is indeed a terrible war & it will be almost a miracle if he comes back unscathed.

The French have been doing well & gaining several miles of strongly entrenched ground near Arras. The English have been held back from following up the French movement by want of shells & high explosive. It is an abominable shame that the Government did not organize our industries sooner, both here & in the Colonies. I believe they are slack even now.

Since the Lusitania was sunk there have been many anti-German riots & shops wrecked & large numbers of the enemy aliens have been interned.

May 26th Wednesday
The great news of the War is that Italy threw in her cause with the Allies on the 24th & proclaimed war against Austria, & Germany has declared war on her. They have 2,000,000 men, & have been preparing for the war since it began last August. Hostilities have begun between it & Austria & Venice has been bombed from Austrian aeroplanes already. I am afraid they will damage it dreadfully with gun fire.

Mother & I went to Shrewsbury on the 20th & I left her there with Auntie & came on here yesterday to join the Haywards. (Here is 2 Harmony Terrace, Studland, near Swanage.) A whole Division of soldiers was being moved from this part to Winchester or France & it made the trains near here very crowded. In one part I had to go 1st instead of 3rd & some had to stand. This is a lovely part of the country, with thatched cottages & beautiful trees, wonderful distances across to Pool[e] & the Isle of Wight, etc. & fine chalk cliffs by the sea. Such a calm & peaceful sea today, only the inevitable mine sweepers at work to remind one of the dreadful conflict raging but a short distance away, those fiends have again used thick clouds of poison fumes & thus gained ground from the British at Ypres.

May 30th Sunday
We have had & have beautifully sunny weather, but cold constant East winds, which will enable the Germans to use their poison gas. The chemical works where they make their poisonous gases at Ludwigshafen on Lake Constance have been bombed heavily by 18 French airmen & several fires & explosions were caused.

There has been a great change in the Government. A Coalition Ministry has been formed of Liberal & Conservative members. Mr. Lloyd George is Minister of Munitions, which seems to give great satisfaction. It is to be hoped he will produce the necessary high explosives before all our brave fellows have been killed for want of them. The casualty lists are dreadful, every day 150 to 200 officers & 1500 to 2000 men. The Dardanelles landing & battles against the Turks have caused great loss of life, chiefly to the Australians & New Zealanders.

We have not heard from Henry since last Sunday, a week ago. But as Mother (at Shrewsbury) is due to get the next letter, I should not hear of it till 1 or 2 days later.

Mr Balfour, Mr Bonar Law & Mr Austen Chamberlain are in the new Ministry. Mr Asquith is still Prime Minister & Earl Grey Foreign Minister. Lord Kitchener is, of course, War Minister.

The Germans have been pushing the Russians back in the East & are surrounding Przemysl. It seems quite possible even that they may retake it. Their artillery & heavy guns are much more powerful than the Russians'. They have also invaded the Balkan Provinces. The Russians expect the War to last a long time & are preparing for the next winter campaign. The "Times" articles by a neutral shew the Germans as thoroughly united & confident that they will not be beaten, even though Italy also has joined the Allies.

We have lost 2 more battleships this week in the Dardanelles, the "Triumph" & the "Majestic". This makes 6 that have been sunk in this part of our operations. Also the auxiliary ship "Princess Irene" has blown up quite suddenly in Sheerness Harbour with its crew & 76 workmen & all perished except one, who thinks he was blown straight out from the centre of the explosion as he was at work on the ship at the time. She was a C.P.R. Passenger vessel & was taken over by the Government for oil fuel.

There has been an appeal issued, asking people not to eat much meat, as the supply is less than usual & it is important to save the milk for the children. We are just having it once, in the middle of the day, here.
No news from Stuart for several weeks.

June 2nd Wednesday – Studland
The first Zeppelin raid over London, so long talked of & expected took place on Monday night. We are not allowed to be told the exact parts of London, 90 bombs were dropped, chiefly incendiary, & several fires were lighted & some damage was done but only 3 fires required fire engines to

extinguish them. Four people were killed & several injured. The killed were, one woman, one man, one child & 1 infant.

The weather was (& is) perfect for Zeppelin exploits, sunny & still, though not hot, at night. In fact there have been slight frosts. Henry writes that he is sleeping every other night in a shell-swept village ½ a mile from the firing line, does not even remove his boots & gaiters. "Hughey" takes the other days.

June 6th Sunday

The news from the Eastern side of the theatre of war has been very bad this week. Przemysl has been recaptured by the Germans & Austrians & they are pressing on towards Lemberg. This setback of the brave Russians is entirely due to the superior artillery, especially big guns & great supplies of ammunition of the Germans. They fired 200,000 shells in 2 hours! The Russians admit that they will for the present be obliged to act on the defensive until England can supply them with munitions & it is feared that the Germans will move large numbers of their victorious troops from the East to the West & the great guns & try to break through the English & French lines, leaving only sufficient troops to hold the Russians in check. It seems most probable & a serious outlook for us, as our supply of high explosive shells is admittedly insufficient. I fear it will very much prolong the war & cause terrible loss of valuable lives, all alas! our best. Conscription has not been brought in even now, & all the slackers & shirkers are allowed to stay at home. Lloyd George says they have sufficient men at present for the equipment which is ready for them. He has been speaking in Manchester to rouse up masters & men to do their best possible work in making shells & munitions.

Stuart is still at Dovercourt.

I heard from Henry last on Wednesday.

June 23rd Wednesday

I have returned home, I came 10 days ago. Mother is still at Shrewsbury & I am to fetch her home next week. I came round by Northwood, where I stayed 5 days & went up to London & saw the Academy & met Surgeon-General & Mrs Jencken at Morleys' Hotel[37] in Trafalgar Square. He has a temporary appointment in London, the Eastern Command. She came up from Colchester the same day we left Studland.

I came home to enable Evans to go home to be with her mother, who is 83 & not well enough to be quite alone in her cottage. So Evans has left us today, after being our devoted & faithful servant for 22 years. We shall miss her terribly. I am writing this quite alone in the house, as Nancy & Price & Imeson & Rags have all gone with Evans to see her off. She had 15 packages & a bicycle! Three of the large packages are following by goods train. Imeson has left his place & is staying here & helping us while looking out for another one. I am very glad of the extra help under the circumstances.

Henry has been having exciting times, having his dressing station set on fire by the shells, & the bombs close to it got quite hot & were thrown into a ditch to cool them. His mackintosh in the dressing station was cut to pieces & he has ordered another. He rushed in between the shelling & seized his possessions & the dressings. His map & map case & cover & bicycle were destroyed. After that he had to have his dressing station in a dug out. There the General asked him to go & see where a shell had fallen & no sooner had he got outside than a piece of shell flew towards him & dropped at his feet. He says they fly about for 1 minute after the explosion.

I am thankful to say that in the last letter he says he is in a town where he has been sent to rest, though personally he prefers the trenches & sleeps better among the shells!

The Zeppelins have raided Hull & Newcastle & killed 40 people at Hull & 16 at Newcastle & injured many. But the papers are not allowed to say much about it. Miss May Place is Lady Superintendent of Ammunition Masters at Elswick & lives at Newcastle & saw the Zeppelins & the bombs dropping.

The placards tonight say a great battle is raging at Ypres.

The Russians are, one gathers, being pushed back & the Germans are nearing Lemberg. Henry says he is convinced there will be a winter campaign & the Russians are preparing for one.

June 27th Sunday

The Germans & Austrians under General von Mackensen have retaken Lemberg, which was taken by the Russians as long ago as September 2nd. Of course they are rejoicing greatly. It will certainly lengthen the war &

cheer our enemies, which is very unfortunate. One must admit that we have not got very far yet in moving the Germans either East or West. On the West they have been using liquid fire against the French, but all the same, they did not make much headway. They say the Germans are to have 18 new Army Corps ready by the end of July. Let us hope our high explosive shells & big guns will also be ready by then!

Henry has had 5 days rest in Estaires, a town North of La Bassée, but today's letter written on the 24th, says he is being sent to the trenches again, a few miles north of La Bassée.

Stuart writes that he is on duty at a Kindergarten in Felixstowe, i.e. training young officers in 10 weeks or less. Our losses each day are terrible, both officers & men. Generally between 100 & 200 officers every day in the Casualty List, & yet so little to show for it!

Evans has had to go home to be with her Mother, after being with us 22 years. A great loss! I am dusting the drawing room every morning to try & do with only 2 maids.

July 10th Saturday

Today there is the cheering news that German South West Africa has surrendered unconditionally to General Botha. He has behaved splendidly & been most loyal. Our force had many difficulties to contend with, the distances were great, one column covered 45 miles in 16 hours, the Germans polluted the few wells there were & at the beginning we were short of equipment. So we shall be no more troubled by the Germans in South Africa.

In the European theatre of war things are much as they were. The Russians have stemmed the Austro-German drive & though they have retreated, their armies are unbroken & were defeating the Austrians in some parts.

The Government have issued a great War Loan, they want £900,000,000. Everyone is asked to contribute, not only the rich, but the working people & servants, etc., all are asked to invest their savings in it. They issue 5/ – vouchers as well as £5 ones. We have done what we can, Mother has put in £300, Henry £300, Imeson £300, all his savings, & Price £5. As I took up £100 of the old War Loan which I only finished paying in April, I have only been able to borrow £100 from Mother's £300, which enables me to convert my old War 3½ % Loan stock into the new Stock at 4½ % on payment of £5.

Tomorrow I will try to write more, now I must mend gloves.

July 22nd Thursday

I was not able to write more on the Sunday & have been too busy ever since. Four days I have left at 2.45 & cycled to Skelton, 3 miles, & spent the afternoon making hay at Skelton Grange[38] to help Delia Place.[39] The weather has been very unsuitable, constant rain, & not one really settled fine day. I find the work sufficiently tiring not to feel inclined to do any brainwork when I get home. Delia has 3 "patriotic lady workers" helping her & living in the house. Two of them are paid a little & the 3rd only gets her keep. Delia gave what they asked.

Henry has applied for a weeks' leave from the 28th, but does not know whether he will get it. Col. Sharpe has his leave & wrote to me from Ilkley, sending 3 spools of photos from Henry's camera to be developed & printed. He asks for the prints. Harry Scott has also applied for his leave on the 28th.

The Russians are being pushed back by the Germans & the latter are near Warsaw & also near, only 5 miles, from the Lublin – railway to the South of it.

Mrs Stour-Fox today suggested it was merely strategy on the part of the Russians to draw the Germans away from their own country & attenuate them. Let us hope it is so. The "Times" does not suggest it, but perhaps they are not allowed to. In the West things are practically stationary & Zeppelin raids have ceased since Lieut. Warneford, V.C., exploded one of them & burned it in mid air.

There has been a splendid victory in South-West Africa by General Botha who drove the Germans to the furthest railway terminus, by long rapid marches & the enemy surrendered unconditionally. I wrote a poem "Victory" about it & sent it to the Yorkshire Herald. Unfortunately (or perhaps fortunately!) they printed it in the Sunday edition & very few people saw it. Still, it is encouraging to have it printed at all.

The War Loan so far as is generally known amounts to at least £600,000,000 which is a hitherto unheard of sum & very satisfactory.

Mother took up £300 & Henry took up £300. All I could manage was to convert £100 of the Old War Loan onto the New & I have got Mother to lend me £100 out of her £300 to do so. Stuart also has taken up £100 & £30 through the Post Office. Imeson put all his savings £300 in & Price £5. So our household alone has put in more than £1,000. Not so bad!

July 26th Monday

The Russians are being driven back by the Germans & Austrians, but especially by the Germans in the North who are getting very near Warsaw. The factories from there have been removed further into Russia particularly the munition factories & the government are helping to transport the machinery & plant. South of Warsaw the enemy are within a few miles of the important railway Lublin-Cholan, though they are not in possession of any part of it & the Russians are defending it valiantly. The fighting has been very desperate.

The West side is practically in status quo. Henry is stationed with his Ambulance between Poperinghe & Ypres. He hopes to come home on leave in about 10 days.

My days are very fully occupied at present. In the morning I dust the drawing room (the former Consulting room), then attend to the canary & the plants, after that do any necessary shopping or business & then I try to get some of the ½ yearly bills reckoned up for Henry. Although Dr Micklethwait is doing the work, he has asked me to send out the Bills, as he does not know what to charge. Then I try, quite in vain! to have luncheon at 1pm. It is always nearer 1.30, rest for about ½ hour & cycle off to Skelton to help Delia with her haymaking. She is alone in charge of the farm, as her brother Arthur is in the A.S.C. in France. Of course all the young labourers are gone too. She has 3 "Patriotic" Lady workers staying in the house & helping her, 2 for wages, 1 for nothing. Of course she is glad of any extra help. I stay till about 7. The weather is most trying for it. Three times I have returned in the rain & not once have we had a whole sunny afternoon. The hay crop is very scanty & much damaged by the constant drenchings.

This morning, to my horror, I found that all Henry's suits lying in his drawers, had moths in them, some had holes from them, especially his favourite & best cycling suit. Very annoying.

Last Sunday some of my verses, called "Victory", were printed in the Sunday edition of the Yorkshire Herald. They were about Gen. Bothas' splendid victory in South-West Africa. Scarcely anyone seems to have seen them. I sent them 5 days before & hoped to have had them printed in a weekday edition.

August 1st Sunday

The news from Russia is very serious. By bringing up great masses of men, guns & ammunition the Germans, on the North, & the Austrians & Germans on the South, have forced back the valiant Russians, who are not so well supplied with guns & ammunition. The enemy are in places in possession of the 2 important railway lines from Warsaw, to Petrograd. Also a large cavalry force under von Falkahein[40] has invaded the Baltic Provinces & is threatening the railway line to Petrograd in the North.

Under these circumstances the Russians have decided to evacuate Warsaw & retire to a line of defence further East, 120 miles from Warsaw.

It is a great triumph for the enemy & will doubtless lengthen the War very much. But if all goes well, the Russian Army will be still intact & able to take the offensive when the necessary guns & ammunition is ready for it. Though, as the summer is so nearly over, it is doubtful if they can do much before next spring, and meanwhile it may be that the Germans will bring over millions of men & thousands of guns to the West & try to force their way to Calais or Paris. We seem quite unable to do more than hold them, I suppose on account of want of guns & shells. It has been a most disappointing year on the West, to my mind.

Henry has been very busy behind the lines at Ypres, making great Baths for the men. They have proved a great success. He can bath 100 men per hour & hopes to extend it to 200 soon. Each man gets clean hot water & clean clothes. Henry has had to arrange the Laundry of 50 women at a place 8 miles away. He has had to do nearly all the planning for the baths himself, as the engineers are all wanted in the trenches. He has asked for goggles (motor) & a scarf as he has sore eyes & a stiff neck from so much motor driving in getting & arranging things for the Baths. He enclosed a letter from Stuart, which tells how he & another officer have been ordered to organise regiments of soldiers who are too disabled for active service, to do garrison duty. Where, is a secret, but possibly India. General Rundle[41] paid them a surprise visit & was much pleased with the progress they had made.

I have a weeks' holiday from haymaking before Delia Place cuts her 12 acre field. The weather is still rainy. Heavy showers & thunder today & close air.[42]

August 11th Wednesday

The German Armies have closed in on Warsaw from West, South & North & the Russians have been obliged to retire from it in order to preserve their Armies intact. They have effected a steady & orderly retirement back to a new front 120 miles East of Warsaw & their lines have nowhere been pierced. It has been a terrible disappointment for them, to have to retire & give up Warsaw, the 3rd city in Russia, with 900,000 inhabitants, but they are not depressed & say they are coming back again & will drive the Germans out of Russia & back to Berlin. Most of the inhabitants left the city, only the Poles stayed behind, & all the copper & brass & bronze & everything that would help the Germans, was removed & carried away into Russia in a great number of trains. Of course it will lengthen the war, but the enemy have lost an enormous number of men, which they cannot replace and when the Allies get their ammunition & guns, their turn will come.

Yesterday we heard that the Zeppelins had attacked the East Coast and come as near York as Selby. Some people in York were awakened by the noise, among others our housemaid, Nancy, but she did not know what it was. The fire engines were got ready & the hooter was very nearly sounded.

Mother heard today from Henry. He is very busy with his Baths, & finds great difficulty in obtaining the necessary timber. He is building an ironing shed. He may get leave about the 23rd.

August 22nd Sunday

A long interval, but I have been busy in the evenings lately, making covers against flies, of gauze & beads. I made 3 for Henry & then gave them to Stuart, but I must explain how that came about. Last Monday & Tuesday Mrs Mends began a series of Working Parties from 2.30–6 to make Sandbags. She has 2,000, & wants 3,000 more to make up 5,000 to send to the W. Riding Division. As it was too rainy for haymaking, I went & helped. I found several friends, Miss Harrison and the 2 Miss Ottleys, the Forbes-Dicks etc. It was a busy scene & we had a number of the poorer women sewing up the bags, as fast as they could be cut out & folded in ready for them. I acted as shopwalker, collecting the finished bags & setting new women on to work, etc. It was tiring & on Tuesday evening I had come back & taken Rags for a short walk & was feeling glad that my day's work was done & gathering a few ripe plums in the garden, when Price came running out with a telegram. It was from Stuart, to say he would arrive home at 9pm & leave again the next day. Nancy was out for the evening, so Price & I had to turn to & get the spare room ready. She lighted the fire to air the bed & I fetched sheets & towels from the Bathroom & we laid the carpet between us & were ready for him by 8.45. He arrived with no luggage whatever, just as he was. He had only heard at 12am that day that he might have to leave in 48 hours, so came up to town to get some drill uniform, as there was not time to get it made by Flight as he had intended. He had to get some shabby 2nd hand stuff. Then he decided to come & say goodbye to us, as, once out, he will probably not return until after the end of the war. So it came about that I gave him my 3 fly covers & have had to spend 3 more evenings in making 3 more for Henry & have not written up my Diary. On Wednesday morning Stuart & I sallied out shopping & bought him a valise & 2 blankets & 2 thin shirts & 4 collars & 2 pairs of sheets, all of which Mother presented him with. She also gave him some towels & pillow cases. He had to leave again by the 12.15 for Kings X. I saw him off. I heard from him today that after all they are not leaving until the 26th, when they will have all their equipment ready.

No letter from Henry since last Sunday. I have finished my Haymaking at Skelton. Last Friday the last load was loaded by little Henry! 6 years old. So short of workers were we at the end!

There have been several Zeppelin raids on the East Coast. No places are mentioned in the papers, but privately I hear they have been at Dover & damaged the Lord Warden Hotel & at Parkstone near Dovercourt where 30 people were injured, but none killed.

August 29th Sunday

We are puzzled & rather anxious about Henry. He wrote, in a letter I had from him last Monday, that he had applied for leave & expected to arrive home on the 28th or 29th, but would write again later. He wrote from the front trench, where he was taking another man's work & had not been able to take his clothes off for 8 days & felt very dirty, as the mud was so thick that it splashed above his borrowed gum boots. He said it was a "very hot spot" & he had forgotten his smoke helmet.[43] Since then, we have heard no more from him & he has not appeared.

Stuart left last Wednesday in the "Empress of Britain" for Malta or Lemnos. His regiment is called the 1st Garrison Batt. Essex Regt.[44] They were intended for India, but India refused to have them. It seems a poor thing that Stuart should be sent off for garrison duty with a number of physical incapables, after 20 years in the army & only 3½ years on the Reserve in between.

The Allied Aircraft have been very active & damaged a German poison factory & various railway stations & our fleet have bombarded Zeebrugge & destroyed at least one submarine & injured some big guns.

The Russians are still retiring in order & their fleet drove the German fleet away from Riga.

September 1st Wednesday

Still no letter from Henry. We cannot understand it & are very uneasy. We intend sending a telegram to him tomorrow, unless we hear from him.

September 5th Sunday

Henry never answered our telegram, although Mother prepaid the answer, nor has he written. We were both very miserable & thought some dreadful thing might have happened to him until Saturday (yesterday) morning, when Mrs Micklethwait rang me up at 8.30 on the telephone & said they had seen young Hassle, who was home on leave & he saw Henry on his way. So I rang him up & he told me he saw Henry on Monday, & that he was well & with the Ambulance 5 or 6 miles behind the firing line & enjoying his work. It is too funny of him not to write. Even the Micklethwaits were uneasy about him, as he wrote to them from the trenches also. The relief of knowing he was all right was immense.

There has been a great landing of our troops, chiefly Australians & New Zealanders, on the Gallipoli Peninsula. They took the Turks by surprise by landing at Suvla Bay & so were able to establish themselves on the shore. Since then they have stormed a hill, Achi Baba, & almost gained the crest, but were not able to maintain their positions. The fighting has been most fierce on both sides, with a reckless disregard of life & the losses have been dreadful. The battle lasted 4 days. It is so sad to see the long list of Casualties in the Dardanelles. Mrs Starkey's nephew, Lieut. Henty (Australian) has been killed & young Jalland is reported missing. He was with the 6th Yorkshire Regiment.

September 16th Thursday
Henry wrote after a fortnight. He's all right & with the Ambulance behind the firing line. He is coming home on leave on Monday.

September 27th Monday
Henry left us this morning to go back to Poperinghe. I saw him off at the station. It seems very quiet & dull without him.

He arrived on Tuesday morning at 9.30 & ready for breakfast, after travelling all night. He looks rather thinner but very well & healthy & brown. He is still much occupied with the Baths & had to go & see Lord Scarboro' & General Mends next door at the Territorial Headquarters about plans, etc. as they are going to send him out an asbestos building for the Baths for the winter.

We put in an advertisement for him in the Bazaar, Exchange & Mart, before he came for a pair of Zeiss field glasses & he has bought a splendid pair of 8 magnifying power, real beauties, which look quite new in a very nice case. He wants them particularly to observe the aeroplanes with, as he cannot see if they are German or not. His tunic was quite worn into holes, inside & out, & his breeches also required patching. Fortunately he had new ones of each here ready to put on. He tells us the English are very short of ammunition, but the French gunners are excellent & have plenty of shells.

The news this morning is wonderful & most cheering. There has been a forward move on the whole or most of the Allies' line in the West & the French have moved forward along a length of 17 miles to a depth of from 1 to 2¾ miles & the English on a front of 5 miles have pushed forward 2,000 to 4,000 yards.

The Russians also are doing better & driving back the Germans & Austrians at several places.

Stuart has written & sent us a copy of his diary. He is at Lemnos, in sight of the flashes of the guns in the Dardanelles at night.

October 8th Friday
There have been new developments with regard to the War in the Balkans. Bulgaria under King Ferdinand, who is partly a German, has mobilised & the Entente Powers have broken off negotiations with her, as she has declined

to reply to Russia's note demanding an explanation of her mobilisation. The rumour is that she is going to attack Servia on one side, while Germany attacks her on the other. Germany has 400,000 men on the Serbian border. The Allies have replied by landing a large force at Salonika. The Serbs have a railway line from there to their country, which, by a previous Treaty, they may use as they choose. Romania & Greece are in a state of armed neutrality & one cannot tell what further development may take place there.

We have heard again from Stuart. He has been a month at Lemnos & has had no mail from us, although I wrote the day after he left England & sent him a parcel of pyjamas.

The Russians are holding their own & on the West, the Allies are consolidating their recent gains. The Casualty Lists have been very long lately, 100–200 officers each day. Major Monteith of the 2nd Bedford Regt. is killed.[45] Stuart knew him well & stayed at Moniaive with him some years ago.

October 17th Sunday

I have not bought a paper today, but on the placards I saw "Terrific fighting in Servia". The Germans are attacking all along the Danube & the Bulgarians are invading her from the East. It is supposed that the English & French are coming to help Servia via Salonika, but I do not know whether they are really there in any sufficient force.

There has been another raid over London & on the East Coast about 3 days ago. There were 56 killed & 114 injured. There was a fleet of hostile airships. Some returned flying over Holland, to the great indignation of the Dutch.

November 28th Sunday, "Nantgoch" Trapp[46]

A long interval! But there has been no fighting of any consequence on the Western front for since I wrote last, on account of the terrible mud. Henry says "the mud is something awful, it is ankle deep wherever you go & a foot deep in some places". There is also little news from Russia, but what there is, is good. The Russians are holding their own & the Germans have been unable to take Riga or Dvinsk, in spite of great efforts & big losses. The chief fighting lately has been in poor little Servia. They have been most plucky, have refused to make a separate peace with Germany & have been driven from quite ¾ of their country by Germans & Austrians from the North & Bulgarians from the East. The French have come from Salonica in the South & have helped the Servians against the Bulgarians & pushed the latter back somewhat. But their army & all supplies have to come up by a single line of rail from Salonica, which makes things very difficult for them. The English force has apparently not yet been in action, but has established a large base camp at Salonica & is bivouacking there, presumably until sufficient guns & stores are landed. They say there is now 150 stiff miles along which they will have to push the Germans back. We always seem to leave things to fate & suddenly wake up when the harm is done, instead of preventing it. Another terrible waste of valuable lives & time.

Things are almost stationary at the Dardanelles & our Casualty Lists lately have been small.

Henry paid us a short visit. He came home Nov. 3rd & left again on the 6th. It was on business in connection with the Baths & he spent much time with Lord Scarboro', who is the head of the Territorial Association & with Mr Brierly, the architect. On Thursday he wired for extension of leave & getting no reply from Col. Legge he had to leave on Saturday at 6.30am. We all got up at 5am to see him off. I went with him to the station, a beautiful morning. When he got back he found that the wire had not reached Col. Legge until Saturday evening, & the latter was much annoyed.

I have been staying here for a fortnight as my digestion has been very troublesome for some months & Henry, when he came over this last time, & Mr Campbell, both said I ought to have a change of air. So I have been staying with Evans & her mother in their cottage & have had beautiful sunny, frosty weather. Miss Ottley the Younger, has stayed in the house with Mother, meanwhile.

December 12th Sunday

The Germans & Austrians & Bulgarians have practically overrun the whole of Servia. They have entered Monastir, the last important stronghold. The unfortunate Servians, army & inhabitants, are fleeing into Albania & Montenegro, pursued by the conquerors, who claim to have captured many prisoners, guns & war material. The French & English entrenched themselves in good positions near Strumnitza, but the Bulgarians attacked in force & have obliged them to retreat further South, partly, probably, to prevent the single line of railway to Salonica being cut by the Bulgarians. The Serbian army is still said to number 200,000. Of course there has been an appeal for the poor Serbians. I have sent a few old clothes.

The English have been marching on Baghdad for some months & were getting close to it, when they were attacked by a large force of Turks & forced to retreat to Kut-el-Amara, 100 miles from Baghdad.

So the news just now is very unsatisfactory. Yesterday was the last day for the men to enlist under Lord Derby's voluntary scheme.[47]

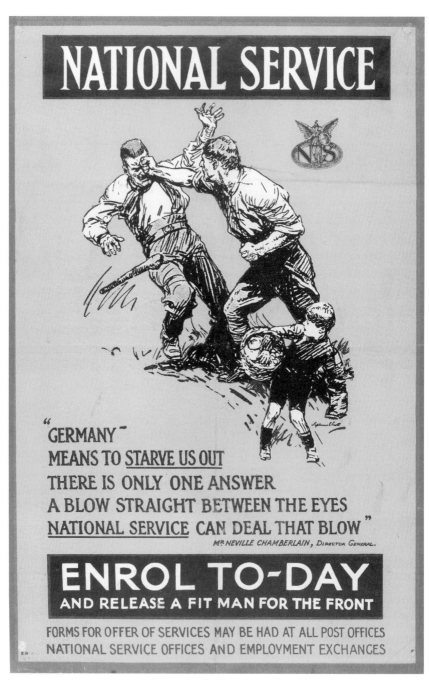

Figure 43: Recruitment poster from early 1917, highlighting the totality of the war and the use of hunger as a weapon, in place from the unrestricted U–boat campaign begun in 1915. A Ministry of Food was established in 1916. (*Royal Pavilion & Museums Brighton & Hove*)

Chapter 10

Mabel Goode's Diary of the Great War: 1916

May 3rd 1916

This year had a sad beginning. My dear Mother died on January 27th after a fall & a short illness, only 10 days in bed. Henry got home, by the mercy of God, just in time for her to recognise & speak to him. My telegram could not have reached him in time. Stuart, who was at Moudros in the Isle of Lemnos, had a vision of her looking 30 years younger, just about the time she died.

We buried her in York Cemetery. Fred Hayward came & helped me & I shut up the house for a month. I spent 2 weeks with Aunt Alice at Shrewsbury, 1 week with cousins Amy & Ethel at Walton by Clevedon & 1 week in Studland with Joan Goode[48] as my companion. Now I am living home alone & have only Price for my servant.

Henry keeps well & writes cheerfully. He is somewhere near Amiens & behind the firing line. Stuart is at Ismailia.[49]

Last night (May 2nd) we had the Zeppelins over York. I was just reading Prayers (10pm) when the gas went down & got so low, I had to guess the words at the end. I looked out & found the street in darkness & the trams stopped running. Price & I turned off all the gas we had on & I tried to turn the meter, but it was too stiff. Then I went up to my room to get a warm coat & she fetched coals in. I also took down Rex's brush & biscuit & candles. I thought that very likely they would not really come over York. But they say that they followed the River & then a train, which ought to have stopped. When I got down to the basement, Price called me to come & listen at the open scullery door & sure enough; we heard the loud thud-thud of the great engines, apparently passing overhead & the flashlights flashed out, but we did not see the Zeppelin. I took Price to the little recess by the wine cellar, where we were away from any glass & before we got in, Crash! The bombs began to fall. Several loud ones made the back door rattle & shake & alarmed Price a good deal, but she was really very brave & quiet. Rex barked furiously. Presently we heard the fire engines tearing by, a motor one & a horse one, galloping.

In a few minutes the crashes ceased & we came into the kitchen & stayed there till 12.30, listening now & then at the open scullery door. But we heard nothing more of them & decided to go to bed, as I did not think it likely that they would venture to return, especially as I knew we had several aeroplanes on Knavesmire.

This morning, on opening the paper, I was very sorry indeed to see that Ned Berry had "died of wounds". I heard from Mrs Berry that he was in Mesopotamia & that they were very anxious & sad as he was almost the only officer left. Such a promising young fellow & their only child.

I cycled round & looked at the wrecked homes after breakfast & doing my housework. Nearly all are little two storey houses. Many are wrecked in various parts of York & very sad to see, I have heard for certain that 6 people were killed & of course there are more. Nunthorpe Hall was set on fire by incendiary bombs & all the wounded had to be removed. The fire was soon got under. No damage was done to any other large building of importance.

Later. There were at least 12 people killed & 28 injured

July 9th
The Great Push has begun. On all sides the Allies are pressing upon the Germans. The Russians & Italians on the East have captured several hundred thousand Austrians. On the West the French & British have advanced simultaneously after a terrific bombardment of 5 days. They have taken 20 villages & more & advanced their line 2 or 3 miles in parts.

Henry has moved, but I don't know where to, except that he has sent me 3 cards of Albert & he writes in his letter, dated July 2nd "My diet is bully beef & biscuit, we cannot get bread". So I presume he is near the firing line. I have made him several fruit & seed cakes & sent them out to him.

The fighting is not quite so severe now as it was on the 1st & 2nd of July, as our men & the French are consolidating their positions, which the Germans have lost & been unable to regain. Stuart is at Zagazig.[50] It is 100° in the shade there now.

Personally, I have taken this cottage, Rose Cottage, Aislaby, Sleights, S.O. for June & July.[51] The weather is very bad. Cold & misty, foggy the first 6 weeks.

July 30th Sunday

On the 13th I got a notice from the War Office that Henry had been slightly wounded. It said "Regret Capt. H. N. Goode was wounded slightly July 8th. Remains at Duty". He first wrote that a stone had struck him on the neck from the explosion of a shell, but "done no damage". By degrees it comes out that the stone knocked him down & he was dazed for some time & his elbow was injured. I don't yet know which arm. He can't get bread, only biscuits & bully beef, so I make cakes & send him some every week & last week I sent him 2 Hovis loaves with the fruit cake.

Besides the cooking, I have been haymaking, now the weather is finer & warm, for, first, the Richardsons, who have only one meadow, & latterly, for Mrs Jackson, who is a widow with 3 small children & has 3 meadows. That, also, is finished now.

The Big Push is doing well for the Allies. British, French & Russians are all pressing back the Germans & Austrians. The British have gained 24 square miles of strongly fortified ground from the Germans in France & continue to advance, in spite of desperate resistance & heavy counter attacks.

August 20th Sunday

On the evening of August 9th, at Rose Cottage, Aislaby, I said to Price that it was a splendid night for Zeppelins. I awoke in the night & heard distant crashes. Zepps' surely, thinks I, & I jumped out of bed to listen at the window. Sure enough, in a few minutes came more reports. I called gently to Price, in case she was awake & frightened, but she was asleep. So I left her asleep, groped about for a warm coat, as there was a cold wind, & sat listening by the window. For ½ an hour or so, the booms & crashes came at intervals. Then came several crashes, followed by Pop! Pop! "Anti-Aircraft guns" I thought. Presently came a steady humming, growing quickly louder. I decided to go out & see if I could see anything, so I stole downstairs, Rex following, undid the door & went out. It was a still, starlight night. The humming had become a loud throbbing & up there, showing against the stars, was the long, black, threatening shape of the Zeppelin. It was a most thrilling, weird sensation, standing out there by myself & watching it approaching rapidly. I called up to Price, thinking she might be safer outside & warned her not to strike a light. She told me afterwards that she could not think what was the matter & wondered why she must not strike a light. Meanwhile the Zepp passed, apparently exactly overhead. I gazed at it & prayed a silent prayer that it might not drop a bomb just then. By the time Price had found some clothes & come out, the danger was passed & she was much interested to see it going rapidly away towards the East Coast. A few minutes after it got out of sight, we heard several bombs dropped. The postman next day told me four & he thought, at Whitwell Bay. Price & I went back to bed & heard it strike 2am.

That was my first sight of a Zeppelin, from peaceful little Rose Cottage. I wonder if I shall see any more!

The war is going splendidly for the Allies on all fronts, Russian, Italian, French & British. All are pushing steadily forward & capturing many positions.

Henry was very fit when he last wrote & has since sent a pewter litre measure home.

We left Rose Cottage & came home on August 10th Thursday, after being there 10 weeks.

September 29th Friday

We are getting on splendidly with the War & pushing the Germans back on all sides. The English troops are wonderful, nothing daunts them, they go straight on, through gunfire & bullets & wire, so that we have been able to take villages like Combles & Thiepval, which are really fortresses & which the Germans thought quite impregnable. A little while ago we sprang a surprise on the enemy, by our "Tanks", a form of armoured motor car, which can knock down a wall & go through barbed wire & is not affected by machine guns. They have helped us greatly & frightened & horrified the Germans.

They have been Zepping us a good deal lately, but we have brought down 3 of their Zepps, 2 in flames.

We in York had our raid on Monday night. Our warning (gas turned low) came at 10.45. The two maids, Price & Kathleen & I went below, in our coats. I heard the throb of the engines from the scullery door & just afterwards the bombs began to fall. It was very alarming & disagreeable, as we had to be quite in the dark. Kathleen told her beads fervently,[52] while I held on to Rex & suppressed his indignant barks by holding his mouth to. I found afterwards that some of the reports were our anti-aircraft guns firing, but they all sounded like bombs. We sat some time in the kitchen, as the gas was still off & about 12.30 I went to listen at the skullery[53] door & heard some distant reports & presently came louder ones, the raiders were passing over York again. So we retired again to our dugout, but the crashes did not come so close. But one time I heard a fall of masonry after the crash & think it must have been when Dr Lythe's house was struck in Heworth & broken about in two. No lives were lost in the raid, except that one woman died from shock.

Henry writes that he is moving, it seems to a town, & he may get leave. He never received my beautiful birthday cake, very annoying! I sent him his big leather boots yesterday in 2 parcels & hope he will get them both.

In one town, Bolton or Sheffield, the bombs killed 36 people in this last raid.

October 29th Sunday

Henry writes that he expects leave (10 days) in 3 weeks time & proposes spending part of it in London. There will be long dark evenings in London at the end of November, but it is only 5 days. He is in a "château" & very comfortable. So far they have not moved into a town. He says there are only three doctors left with the Ambulance, the others are away with regiments, etc. Major Whally has returned, so Henry is a Captain again instead of Major. He sent me a cheque for £50, as a birthday present, as I told him I was trying to live on my share of our mutual money. I have put by £156 in War Savings Certs. It will give me £200 in 5 years, if left to accumulate. I sold out £200 Victoria Falls to do it.

The War goes very well on the West Front. All German counter attacks are always driven back or smashed up by the Allies' artillery. We have quantities of guns & shells now.

Roumania joined in on the Allies' side some time ago & the Germans & Bulgarians are pushing her rather hard. They have taken Constanza, on the Black Sea & most of the Dobruja including the important railway line and the Danube & they are in possession of several passes in the North between Bulgaria & Roumania. The Russians are helping the Roumanians but so far the Germans have driven them back. It is too wet & muddy now for the Allies to make much progress in the West, though they continue to move forward. Henry says they think the War may last another 2 years. He got the famous Birthday cake after all! Says it was "much appreciated in the mess".

December 10th Sunday

Henry has been home on 10 day's leave. He arrived at 12.30am on Friday night. Nov. [blank]. The only notice I had was a wire from Kings X, which came about 7.30pm. The maids & I set to & we got his fire lighted & aired the bed & put up his curtains & a globe on his gas & we had all ready for him when he arrived & I made him some cocoa to warm him up after his journey. He had been travelling since the day before, except for 3 hours rest on a sofa at Boulogne. He could not find a bed, all were full. The boats were held up one day, on account of loose mines. He looks splendidly fit & has put on nearly a stone, weighs 12st 8lbs. He spent 4 days in York & we settled about Mother's X & Aunties' Legacy. Then we went for one night to Fred at Hemingford Grey.[54] He has made a charming little home out of the "Six Bells". We had a row on the river & went on pm to London, where Mr Jencken had taken 2 rooms for us in their hotel, Morley's, in Trafalgar Square. We had a delightful 3 days there & enjoyed being with the Jenckens, who were very jolly & friendly. We went to the Alhambra, the Criterion & the Playhouse, the Zoo & had Edith to luncheon at the hotel & went together afterwards to see Fred's pictures at the Oil Painters. Henry had to leave by the 8am train on Sunday morning. I got up & went with him to the station, Victoria. On Monday I returned to my lonely house, but was fortunately busy at the Railway canteen from 7 to 10.30 that evening.

In Roumania things have gone very badly. The Germans are in possession of Bukarest & of the oil fields & one Roumanian army of 10,000 has had to surrender. They seem to have been quite unprepared for the German artillery. Hindenburg has been too much for them.

Greece has proved very treacherous. The Royalists prepared a plot & fired on the Allied troops & ill-treated the Venizelists & killed some & put others in prison & a reign of terror prevails. The Allies are blockading Greece, as a punishment.

There has been an upheaval in our own Government. Asquith has had to resign & Lloyd George is Premier & First Lord of the Treasury. I don't trust L.G. but he has great energy & will probably get things done, whereas Asquith was always putting things off. Many ships have been torpedoed & we are feeling the shortage of food & prices go steadily up. With Roumania in German hands, the war may go on another 3 years, apparently. As far as I can see, I shall spend this Xmas alone. I have made Xmas Puddings & sent one each to Stuart & Henry.

Figure 44: Painting by Mabel of the house she lived in at Outgate in the Lake District 1923. It was in this year that she wrote a series of poems celebrating the area.

Epilogue

'At eleven o'clock this morning came to an end the cruellest and most terrible War that has ever scourged mankind. I hope we may say that thus, this fateful morning, came to an end all wars.'
David Lloyd George, British Prime Minister (1916–22)

An uncertain finish

And so the diary ends. Mabel began writing knowing that the war would be the most important event to take place in her life, making the fact that she stopped writing prematurely all the more intriguing. Truthfully, we will never know why Mabel stopped writing her diary, what led her to put down her pen and not take it up again. The fact that no explanation is offered indicates both that the diary was probably for Mabel's own use, as she would not need to leave an explanation for herself, and also that this end was not planned or sparked by one event in particular. All we have to go on in trying to understand why Mabel stopped writing is what was recorded in her diary at that time. Mabel could not write what she wanted to write: a string of decisive British victories and a quick end. What the diary tells us is a story of gradual disengagement. As the vicissitudes and horrors of war became increasingly apparent and, eventually, even personally threatening, so her eagerness to capture the unfolding of this lengthening, stagnant and ugly conflict weakens, and ultimately fades. Mabel's diary records a lengthening war; a war which evolved into a conflict without precedent, transformed by modern technology and political intransigence into something totally unexpected. The lengthening war extended beyond Mabel's desire to record it, continuing for another two years after she ceased writing.

A change of plans

Mabel lived a long life after the war. Aged 46 when the war ended, she had 36 years to reflect on it: to live first in the uneasy peace it created, then through the tumult of the Second World War, and into the early Cold War austerity that followed.

At the time of writing, Mabel would not have imagined living through those thirty-six years by herself. By the start of the war in 1914, she was already 42 and Henry was 44; both seemed a little old for marriage. It was expected by Mabel, and supposed generally, that she and her brother would continue to live together. According to family understanding, the plan for the siblings was reinforced on their mother's deathbed in 1916 when she made it clear to Henry that she wished for him to take care of Mabel permanently. The entry on 3 May 1916 records this meeting but does not state what took place: 'Henry got home, by the mercy of God, just in time for her to recognise & speak to him'. However, Henry instead refused his mother's wish and announced his intention to marry. The war seems to have changed what he wanted out of life or brought to the surface deep-seated desires.

As many in their mid-forties may tell you, it is one thing to want to marry and another to be able to do so. The death and wounding of millions of young men changed who was considered eligible and how eligible they were. Shortly after the war in 1919, Henry married Rosetta Shann, twenty-six years his junior. Henry and Rosetta had known each other for a number of years before Henry proposed; Rosetta's father was Dr Shann, who had his consulting room in the same building of St Leonards as Henry, so was well known to the family. Henry and Rosetta exchanged a number of love-letters while they were courting. We know from similar letters and her personal 'Roll of Honour' that Rosetta had had several potential husbands lost in the trenches. It was not unheard of for a man to marry at 48, but Rosetta was only 23 when she chose to become Henry's wife. Given that Rosetta must still have been coming to terms with the deaths of suitors her own age, and that her marriage to Henry took place so soon after the Armistice, it seems likely that the war did play a role in Rosetta's decision to accept Henry's proposal.

Figure 45: Photo of Mabel (extreme left), Rosetta (left) and Henry (centre) with their children, probably taken in 1923. The war changed Mabel's plan to live with her brother.

It is an odd, and perhaps cruel, turn of fate that the deaths of the First World War and the pressures of that conflict led to (or at the very least helped) the survival of this line of the Goode family. I have great certainty in saying that I would not be here, if it were not for the war and the loss of so many young men which assisted the marriage of Henry and Rosetta. (Lasting forty years, the marriage was successful.[1] Figure 45 shows the couple and their children, as Mabel looks on.)

Naturally, this decision to marry meant that Mabel, having assumed that her brother would look after her and live with her for the rest of their lives, now found her plans in tatters. The unease of the situation was painfully obvious. Mabel chose to stay in the family house and live with the newly-wed couple for the best part of a year after their marriage, until the first child was on the way.

Politics and the vote

What the war took with one hand, it gave with another. The war had the power to destroy relative certainties, both in one's private and public life: just as it helped an unlikely marriage, so it greatly aided the cause of women's suffrage. It is remarkable to think that Mabel, only three generations back from new voters today, was in the first wave of women in Britain who could vote in a General Election.

There is a tendency in history to see progress as inevitable. As time marches on, so does fairness, development and justice among humanity as a whole. What we lose, in taking this view, is far greater than the optimism we gain. The debate around women's votes was both complex and adversarial. People aligned themselves with one side or the other for a number of reasons. Impressive figures such as Gertrude Bell threw their weight behind the Women's National Anti-Suffrage League (set up in 1908), an organisation which actively campaigned to stop the suffragettes in their tracks. This movement grew in power when the women's and men's leagues merged in 1910 to create the National League for Opposing Women's Suffrage.

By 1912 this group had attracted the support of the serious political heavyweight Lord Curzon (former Viceroy and Governor-General of India). Given such evident opposition and the popular disapproval of many of the radical tactics used by the suffragettes (such as Emily Davison throwing herself under the King's horse in the 1913 Derby, and the use of bombs and arson), without even mentioning the general conservatism of Edwardian Britain, there was certainly no reason for Mabel to expect the vote when it came. In short, to be told as a child in the 1880s that she would get suffrage by 1918 would not have been a blasé comment.

The war had a considerable impact on shifting the grounds on which women could campaign for the vote. Vast swathes of men leaving for the Front combined with the need for all sorts of industries to expand production to support them, meant that the war economy needed new labour, lots of it and fast. It was women who filled the void. Mabel's personal experience of the changing labour market in Britain has already been explored. Her story is typical. Between 1914 and 1916 alone the number of women in formal employment rose twenty-seven per cent.[2] Yet even this figure does not fully convey the dramatic shift, as women not only entered employment for the first time, but they were also undertaking different types of work. Moreover, by only counting women in visible employment, the figures do not capture those who carried out the voluntary or informal work that Mabel (and many like her) undertook. The expansion of female employment during the war played a crucial role in winning the vote for women.

The war brought empowerment as well as employment. The need for men to join the services obliged women to play their part in the recruitment process and made such a part patriotic, giving women a larger role in public life and another claim to helping the war effort. This obligation was certainly felt by Mabel, as seen in the section *Into the fray and the trouble getting there*. Mabel was deeply concerned about Stuart's failure to get to the Front quickly. In the pages of her diary, she worries about the delays, sends clippings from the paper to encourage him to join up and becomes quite critical of his hesitation, being clearly relieved when both he and her other brother are in uniform.

Women were a powerful recruitment aid. This is perhaps best captured in the famous 1915 poster by E. J. Kealey 'Women of Britain say – GO!' The value the government attached to women evoking a man's sense of duty can be illustrated even more clearly in a less well-known poster, also from 1915, called 'To the women of Britain. ... Won't you help and send a man to join the army to-day?' The poster asks, among other questions, the following: 'Do you realise that the one word "GO" from you may send another to fight for our King and Country?' and 'When the War is over and someone asks your husband or son what he did in the Great War, is he to hang his head because you would not let him go?'[3]

What is curious is that at no point in the diary do we see any direct comments on the above developments. It is not even obvious whether Mabel wanted to be able to vote or not, or what party she supported. Alternatively, it could be viewed as curious that Mabel could not vote at the time (and thus had no direct reason to be concerned with politics) and yet she clearly knew, and expected us to know, the names of the politicians of the day. She undoubtedly had her favourites in public life: Lord Roberts' death, in an entry on 15 November 1914, moved her to say 'It is sad.... I am sorry he is gone. There is no one left like him. If only the English would have taken his advice about

National Service, how it would have shortened or prevented this war'. She had those she disapproved of, as an extract from 10 December 1916 shows: 'I don't trust L.G. [Lloyd George] but he has great energy & will probably get things done, whereas Asquith was always putting things off'. Apart from these observations, the only other political comments about the management of the nation come from Mabel's interest in the war effort itself.

The war clearly gave an impetus for women to have a greater political interest in the management of government affairs. Mabel felt it necessary to write critically of the government after certain episodes, as she did on 16 May 1915: 'It is an abominable shame that the government did not organise our industries sooner, both here & in the Colonies. I believe they are slack even now.' It must have been hugely frustrating and distressing for those women who had patriotically encouraged male family-members to enlist, to then feel that the Government was mishandling the conduct of the war and putting men's lives in jeopardy. One can empathise with Mabel as she agonises that her government is allowing key industries to be 'slack' when she, along with the rest of the population, is making sacrifices in the national interest, and her brothers are risking their lives.

Figure 46: Postcard of the hamlet Mabel moved to in 1923 called Outgate.

To be seduced by the idea of progress keeping pace with the passing of time is just that: seduction. Through Mabel we can see that by providing work, patriotic purpose and a sense that the management of Britain was more vital than ever before, the war helped bring about votes for women – which was by no means an inevitability by 1918.

A new home, new values, painting and later life

In 1920 Mabel bought two properties, a house and a nearby cottage. Both were in a hamlet called Outgate in the Lake District, not far from the place to which she had to move when the War Office took over her house in York. (Figure 44 is a postcard of the hamlet, and a painting of the house by Mabel is shown in figure 46.) Her new home, which she called 'The Cottage' was the smaller of the two houses, built in the seventeenth century and without electricity or gas. She let the larger house as a source of income and lived frugally with her maid, Price. Mabel lived here until her death.

It was from around this time that Mabel became a vegetarian,[4] indicating both the strong ideals that she held after the war and that these may have been easier to practice in her newly-found autonomy. There was a London Vegetarian Society in the 1890s (whose membership included Mohandas Gandhi), as well as British, American and international vegetarian societies, so it appears that vegetarianism was an unusual but by no means unknown dietary choice. The most well-known vegetarian of his time was probably the Irish playwright and political thinker George Bernard Shaw (1856–1950) and it seems from family recollections that Mabel was influenced by his example. The family regarded her choice as rather laughable and 'potty' and tended to see it as evidence of Mabel's eccentricity rather than as a decision of principle. There are anecdotes recalling that in World War Two, Mabel had a 'meat eaters' ration book because it had more cheese and eggs and that, in later life, she would eat the bacon on top of the turkey at Christmas but not the turkey itself, carving out (or otherwise) the implications of her principles.

Apart from the diary, Mabel left very few things to the world. The only other legacy left directly from Mabel's hands are the pictures she painted. Having been educated at the Slade School of Fine Art, Mabel was a trained artist from early adulthood. We know very little of her early work, which does not seem to have been preserved. However, we do know that she earned her living as an artist during her later life, and her surviving work seems to have been done after the war in the 1920s and '30s.

Finding herself in unexpectedly independent circumstances and living with only her servant Price, Mabel frequently took winter holidays to Italy, staying in a pension or small hotel (see figure 47 for a holiday photograph from 1927). It is not known when Mabel started these trips or when she ended them, but the family understanding is that her painting was her primary source of funding for such holidays (figure 48 is a typical example). Mabel would paint landscapes of the picturesque scenery in Naples and elsewhere, over the winter, and then sell her pictures in England over the summer, an arrangement that lasted for some years. This suggests that the paintings left in the family were either those that she could not bear to sell, or those that could not be sold. Looking at them now, it is intriguing to see

Figure 47: Mabel feeding the pigeons in Venice, 1927.

Figure 48: Painting of an Italian landscape by Mabel, circa 1920s–30s.

Mabel's images of a country so strongly shaped by the war: Italy, the first nation to embrace fascism.

Mabel's life spanned an extraordinary period of British history. She was born into an Empire on which the sun never set. She spent her childhood in a nation that was merely a year older than her: the Germany of the Second Reich, unified in 1871, a young, self-confident, rapidly industrialising country whose army was the envy of Europe. She returned to a Britain struggling with the Irish Question, women's rights, working-class representation in politics, and the role of the House of Lords. She recorded her experiences of the First World War, an event that led to the end of three Empires, the first Communist government and unprecedented destruction. She moved onto pastures new in the 1920s and 30s, visiting the world's first fascist state and witnessing the hardship of the economic collapse of the Great Depression. She saw the dream of peace shattered, in what must have held more than a hint of déjà vu, as Britain entered into another major war with Germany and fought bitterly against Hitler. Having seen all this, Mabel died in 1954, by herself and with no direct descendants. She was born into a Victorian nation run by Gladstone, where aeroplanes and motor cars were unheard of and the cavalry charge was regarded as a set piece of combat. Just seven years after her death, the first person went into space and the threat of nuclear war hung over Europe.

Figure 49: Photo of Mabel (centre) painting, circa 1930s.

Appendix

Introduction to the Poetry

Both these poems and the love story below were found in Mabel's thin blue notebook from the 1920s. This was discovered in the same chest that held the war diary and can only be assumed to be some of the few documents from Mabel's estate deemed worthy of storing. The notebook itself is more a collection of musings than anything with a coherent theme: it contains artistic observations, funny anecdotes, notes on art and records of financial investments, along with the poems and the love story.

Mabel mentions writing war poetry in the diary and on 9 November 1914 she comments that 'Certainly war inspires poetry. Nearly every day there is some poem in the "Times" & in the "Yorkshire Herald".' We have a record of her RAMC poem being published (see the *And so to the Front* section) and the first two poems in her notebook are specifically about the war and almost certainly both written in 1915.

Mabel records that she wrote 'Victory' for publication in her an entry on 22 July 1915:

> There has been a splendid victory in South-West Africa by General Botha who drove the Germans to the furthest railway terminus, by long rapid marches & the enemy surrendered unconditionally. I wrote a poem "Victory" about it & sent it to the Yorkshire Herald. Unfortunately (or perhaps fortunately!) they printed it in the Sunday edition & very few people saw it. Still, it is encouraging to have it printed at all.

This is a good example of Mabel being upbeat and inspired by the sort of victories she expected to see emerge from the war and conveys an interesting perspective on attitudes about the Boer War and British rule in South Africa. Having a brother who served in the Boer War, probably meant that this theatre of war was both relatively familiar to her and especially close to her heart.

'February 18', written in 1915, is a fascinating poem about the commencement on that day of Germany's unrestricted U-Boat warfare, designed to sink any military and merchant ships heading to Britain. The date effectively represents the start of the German effort to starve Britain and cut it off from the rest of the world, and it quickly led to the total British sea blockade of Germany. The endnotes help add context to the poem but Mabel was making reference to key figures in Germany, what they thought of Britain, what they wanted, and why it would not work.

The four later poems relate to Mabel's new home, 'The Cottage'. This was a small seventeenth century cottage in the hamlet of Outgate in the Lake District, which she bought in 1920 when Henry started his new family and she needed to find somewhere else to live. These poems seem to have all been written in August 1923, in a flurry of creativity inspired by the contrasts, grandeur and sweep of the Lakeland scenery.

Mabel's Poetry

Victory

We met as foes, in fair & manly fight,
So learnt each side the other to appraise
Courage, endurance, strength & prudence right
The Boer unto the Englishman displays.[1]

These foemen worthy of our steel we found
Our noblest leaders & our bravest men
We needed all on that far-distant ground
'Ere we could gain the victory over them.

Yet, having won, we cast the sword aside
And ruled in love, with justice full & free
Knowing the noblest strength is best applied
In giving others all true liberty.

So, in Old England's hour of direst need
When powerful foes would lay her in the dust
Making brute strength their god, & armed greed
Did seek to wrest her lands by robber thrust

Great Botha,[2] loyal to his King, was found

He rose with strength & cast rebellion down
His the first final Victory to win

For this Great Britain thanks her youngest child
Honours & thanks her from a right full heart
Hath she not proved, by blood & sacrifice,
Worthy in our great Empire to take part.

(Feb 18th)

Wily[3] the enemy, crafty & mean
Lying in wait is the sly submarine
Swift the torpedo shoots from the unseen.

Joyful the German, fierce glows his "Hate".
"Perfidious Albion[4] meets with her fate"
"Von Tirpitz[5] destroys her, the 18th's the date."

"Starve shall the English, shaking with fear,
No ships dare venture out, lest we be near
So shall the Kaiser win & "Der Tag"[6] appear".

Scornful the English smile "On ocean foam
Danger & death we meet, as we roam,
Shall a mere German threat keep us at home!"

"Ram we the submarine, evade the torpedo
Rulers of ocean, we fear not the foe,

May God receive our souls, sink we below."

So, all round England, the 17th o'er
Liner & steamer, from harbour or shore
All the proud British ships sailed as before.

Lakeland Poem (Aug 1923)

With its up & downs
With its smiles & frowns
Ho! This is the land for me
Where the mountains stand
all rugged & grand
Round lakes, deep in mystery.

On their sides so steep
Roam the mountain sheep
Alone amid the wild.
How they scamper & run
when they see us come
where the rocks & heather lie piled.

On a windy day
Great shadows play
Hide & seek on the fell sides green
O'er the riven sky
White clouds tear by
With the bluest of blue between.

When the clouds descend
There is rain without end
Brown torrents come foaming down.
The sun bursts through,
The sky is blue,
The smile succeeds the frown.

When the sun shines hot
And the winds are not
You may lie on the heather & sleep.
Or watch the deer
From far or near
On heights, that a stillness keep.

With the dales folk kind
of a gentle mind
'Tis a joy & a pleasure to be.
With its ups and downs
With its smiles & frowns
Ho! This is the land for me.

(Aug 20th 1923)

The winds are blowing
The waters are flowing
There is a scent of new mown hay
The cocks are crowing
All things are growing
The earth is alive today.

My Little Home (Aug 21st 1923)

I've a little, little home
of my very, very own
In the Lake countree!
And wherever I may roam
On the Land, or o'er the sea
There'll be one little spot
That will never be forgot
T'will be that little home
In the Lake countree.

After the Gale (Aug 22nd 1923)

There is music in the mountains
There are voices in the vale
For full are all the fountains
From the greatness of the gale.

The brooks are babbling brightly
Some little liquid song
Could I but catch it rightly!
But it gurgles – & goes on.

Brown becks, in merry madness
Are bursting all their banks
In a rush & roar of gladness
They are telling out their thanks.

Introduction to Mabel's Love Story

This story is titled 'John' and is about what was clearly a profoundly meaningful part of Mabel's life. The narrative covers a period from August to November 1928, when Mabel is just turning 56 years old and 'John' is a couple of years younger. It seems to have been written from the perspective of some eight months later, at a point when Mabel and John are still writing to one another but apparently have not met each other since. The setting is Bibury, a picturesque village in the Cotswolds. John's father had established a trout farm there in 1902.

This little story is a fascinating document on a number of levels. On one level, the story is an unexpected insight into Victorian artistic circles, particularly of the pre-Raphaelites. John's grandfather was a friend of John Keats, his father (Arthur Severn) was a successful watercolour painter, his mother was a cousin of John Ruskin, and John grows up knowing the artists Burne-Jones, Rosetti and Holman Hunt. Mabel and John both know the family of William Watson, a well-known poet, and they share an interest in William Morris and a deep knowledge of the work of John Ruskin. John's family home, Brantwood, was originally the home of John Ruskin and the Severns lived there and inherited it on his death in 1900. By chance, Brantwood is only four miles from Mabel's own home at Outgate.

On another level, it conveys sharply and clearly the interactions between these two individuals, one a middle-aged 'lady artist', the other a gentleman trout-farmer from a well-known artistic family. Trivial conversations are carefully reproduced and fleeting facial expressions described, building up for us a picture of Mabel's stilted, stumbling attempts at friendship and intimacy. Mabel tells of how she felt 'cheated of happy intercourse with men' (it seems, from family anecdote, that Mother did not wish her to marry) and now, on a 'fateful day', when she feels she is 'less shabby than usual', she determines to speak to a man. The initial approach is successful, and Mabel now finds she cannot stop thinking of him. She goes to London but changes her plans and returns; then, 'with my heart in my mouth', she engineers the opportunity to get to know him better. As she tells us, 'That was the first of the four most interesting days of my life.' He invites her to tea: 'my heart nearly failed me – Tea alone with a man I hardly knew! Never had I done such a thing before and I thought how shocked Mother would have been.' Boldly, Mabel determined to 'stick to my freedom and go.' The story takes us through the next three months as poor Mabel contemplates how she may seize 'a life happiness, or even the chance of it' but instead suffers slights, hurt, and 'bitter tears of mortification', as John seems neither to notice or care. The story details carefully what was said, but behind the words Mabel seems unable to perceive motivation: she misreads John, and has no insight into how she is attempting to construct an intimacy that does not exist.

The story also shows us some of the Victorian conventions as they were slowly eroded in the inter-war years. Mabel is independent; she is comfortable travelling around Paris and has been to Venice three times, yet still she expects other people to be shocked that she would go to tea alone with a gentleman. Walking together in the dark, she 'would have liked to have asked to take his arm! but was afraid he might think me forward!' When John changes his boots, she 'looked out of the door, not to embarrass him.' She is distraught when John does not answer her letter, because this is 'not quite polite' but 'I felt that I must forgive him' for his breach of manners 'or what was love worth'. The summit of her relationship is when he 'raised his hat with a smile and I waved my hand. It was one of the happiest moments of my life.'

Mabel's Love Story (1928)

John

I first saw him in church on August 21st, liked the refined voice, but had no idea who he was.

Then I was told by my Hotel table companions that he was the man who owned the trout farm opposite the hotel.

It was not until the next Sunday, August 28th, that my chance acquaintance, Miss Randall, told me his name and that he was a great-nephew of R – [Ruskin]. As R – was an only child, this did not sound correct! But the evident connection between the two aroused my intense interest.

Before I knew his name, he had several times passed over the bridge on his chestnut horse and peered over to try and see what I was painting and looked interested.

Then came the fateful day when I first spoke to him. Miss Emerson had motored over to lunch with me at the Swan Hotel and afterwards taken me to Kelmscott[7]

After she left, about 4:30, I painted the Cottages, Arlington Row[8] and when the light had gone went for a walk up the village and through a gate into the fields. Before this I had thought of writing a story and he was to be the hero. As I walked through the fields, I imagined to myself what it would be like, if it were real – he and I liking each other. Inflamed by the idea and the charm of it and the feeling of having been cheated of happy intercourse [meaning interaction] with men, I determined that if I had the opportunity, I would speak to him. I had on my yellow wool frock and best black hat and felt less shabby than usual and as I passed by the trout farm after the mill, there he was, walking rather quickly with something like a pail in his hand. Determined to carry out my resolution, I looked at him and smiled! He responded with a pleasant 'Good afternoon'.

I said, 'It is a warm day'.

John, 'It is the first day of real warmth we have had.'

I, 'I hope we shall have some more of it.'

John, 'Yes, I hope we shall.'

Meanwhile he had been moving further away and was now too far off, so our conversation ceased and I walked on to the hotel, pleased with the success of my venture and thinking what a very pleasant voice he had.

The next day I was finishing my painting of the Mill Stream and Bridge and John came by on his bicycle with his fishing tackle tied on. He just saw me in passing, but evidently did not recognize [sic] me, in my sketching clothes, as the one who had spoken to him the day before.

Two days later I went to London, to the Club, without having seen him or spoken to him again.

II

When I got to London, I found, to my surprize, [sic] that what had been begun in a spirit of fun and adventure, seemed to be becoming serious. I could take little or no interest in the shops and clothes, usually a great amusement and pleasure. Instead I felt him near me and saw him.

I had intended going on to Paris the following week, but so strong and insistent was my feeling about John that I decided to go back to Bibury, get to know him and then with real contact the feeling would I thought probably pass away. I made the outward excuse that the Paris Studios might not be open until later.

So, on September 8th, I returned to Bibury, to the Hotel. That afternoon I did not see him.

On Friday, the next day, I still looked in vain to see him on the trout farm, and began to fear that I had had my journey and expense for no purpose.

On Saturday morning I wrote a letter in the sitting room window which commands the mill entrance to the trout farm and to my joy a figure came walking quickly down the road, straight towards the hotel – John, at last! I got my first near view of him and liked his quick upright walk. So I had not come in vain and I determined to take the next possible opportunity of speaking to him, making the excuse (and partly also a true reason) of asking permission to paint on his farm.

So after the Service on Sunday evening, I managed to come out of church side by side with him. He gave me a modestly enquiring glance to see if he knew me and evidently did not remember ever having seen me before.

With my heart in my mouth, I seized my opportunity and spoke 'Mr Severn, do you mind if I go into your trout farm to paint?'

His face lighted at once and with a look of keen interest he told me to go anywhere I liked. He told me there were chairs in the little Hatching House and even a sketching umbrella at my disposal. I told him that I also came from and lived in the Lake District and only 4 miles from his house [Brantwood]. I tried to make Lady Watson a tie between us as a mutual acquaintance, but this was a failure, as he had not known her himself and said that she and his father had not hit it off happily together when she and Sir William[9] spent the winter in his father's London house. But presently he looked up at me with a look full of charm and expression and said 'It is so interesting to know you come from that part.' I responded with a friendly smile and we walked on chatting happily, as far as the little gate into his domain, some way past the hotel, and there we parted, as he appeared to be going in. That was the first of the four most interesting days of my life.

The next day, Monday, I went up the village to buy some lemons and met John coming down the hill. I said, 'I never told you my name yesterday' and he said 'Do tell me'. And after I had, he said he had been thinking that the best way would be for him to take me over the farm and show me the best points of view. I quite agreed (naturally!) and said I would join him shortly. So I got my lemons and met him near the hotel and told him I wanted to leave a little parcel in the Hotel first. He said 'Certainly, I will wait for you here'. And he remained leaning over the parapet of the little bridge until I returned. We went towards the little gate and he said 'Do you mind a pipe?' (He was smoking one.) I said, 'No, I like it.' We entered and he showed me where to cross the little streamlets and took me up to the hedge near the Mill and asked if I knew the Collingwoods. At one crossing he said 'Do you want a hand?' But I did not take it. I mentioned I would like to see a kingfisher and he said he could probably get one for me. I said (rather pertly!) that I could hardly keep it for a pet. So he said 'Perhaps a stuffed one.' (But so far no kingfisher has appeared. I rather thought one might have at Xmas!) Then he told me his father painted and he had some of his pictures and with an obvious effort and fear of refusal he suggested that he could show them to me if I would come and have tea with him. I felt somewhat bold and venturesome but felt 'In for a penny, in for a pound' and said 'I should love to come.' He said would I come that day or Tuesday? We decided on Tuesday. I thought it would be nice to have it to look forward to.

On Tuesday, my heart nearly failed me – Tea alone with a man I hardly knew! Never had I done such a thing before and I thought how shocked Mother would have been. It was raining and I felt I could easily send that as an excuse. But when I mentioned what I was going to do to Mr and Mrs – at my table at meals, they did not seem shocked and I decided to stick to my freedom and go.

It was raining, so I went in my dark blue suit, light blue jersey and old grey felt hat. I arrived punctually and the door was opened by a pleasant-faced woman who showed me upstairs and said he had come in and would be down very soon. It was a pleasant room, though not large, and hung round with pictures, mostly water colours. I had been a little doubtful whether it was to be just us two or more, but a glance at the tea tray settled it – just two cups! I took off my mac and going outside the room to put it down, I met him just coming in. He had on a nice rough suit of reddish brown frieze which suited him.

He rang for the tea and began to talk about the pictures and put me in an easy chair near the fire and near the table and tea tray and he sat near and poured out the tea. We had home made cake and white scones, nothing brown. It was very comfy and pleasant. I asked him about Ruskin, what he was really like, when he was alright,[10] and he said 'Very nice and liked being read to' and took an interest in things and asked him about his fishing etc.

I told him I had been to Kelmscott and did he know William Morris? He said no, but he had known most of the Pre-Raphaelites – Burn-Jones very well when he (himself) was a lad and when he told him his school troubles, B-J laughed at him; also he knew Rosetti and Holman Hunt. For the first time then I discovered the colour of his eyes, a delightful blue. He poured out the tea very sympathetically and himself offered to fill up my cup with hot water for my second cup. He talked about the pictures, which were nearly all painted by his father, but said I must not get up to look at them until after tea. He told me his father was 86 and still painted. I said 'But what about his eyes?' And he answered 'They are still perfect!'

After tea we went round the room and he told me about the pictures. He evidently loved them all and knows a lot about painting. He criticized them keenly but appreciatively. I remember a large one of Venice and I said I had been there 3 times and he said 'Well done!'

Some were of rivers in Scotland where he had fished while his father painted. He said his father was a very quick painter. One was of the trout farm, a lovely foreground of poppies, looking from the little hatching house towards the bridge. I thought all very clever. He rather seemed to say that his father had not done quite as well as he might have, had he worked harder. His father was in London. He said his father was a splendid critic and amusing to go to the Academy with, as he held forth so loudly that quite a lot of people followed him to hear his remarks about the pictures. I was surprized to find that he had only quite the cheap (Everyman's) edition of Ruskin's works. He said he had had one good one and his mother sent for it and sold it. But, he said, 'I thought it was a present'. I thought it a great shame and that his mother must have been lacking in kind feeling. He said he specially liked the 1st Volume of Modern Painters and the Seven Lamps of Architecture. I told him I had a nicely bound edition of the latter that my mother had given me and he seemed pleased. After the pictures we sat down again and agreed about the evil of betting and gambling, but I can't remember what began that. I came at 4.30 and left at 6.30.

He came down to the gate with me and said, rather worriedly, 'I must be off'. I thanked him and said I had enjoyed it very much and he said 'It was very good of you to come'. It had now left off raining, so I went to the Hotel and fetched my sketching things. On the way I passed Mr and Mrs – who were staying at the Hotel, and they asked me how I had enjoyed my visit and I replied enthusiastically that it had been most interesting. I went into the T.F. [trout farm] and settled down to sketch at a point I had chosen in the morning. I only began a small one, as the weather was so uncertain. I had got it drawn in and begun to colour it, when J. [John] came along. 'You have chosen a beautiful subject,' he said, 'and I think it is so clever how you have got in that fine old house beyond the mill.' I think he asked me again what my name was and said, 'Perhaps we shall meet again in the Lake District.' I said I hoped we should. Then he remarked rather worriedly, 'I have got to show those people round so I must go', referring to some people who had just come into the T. F. I did not stay much longer and that sketch of the Mill is still unfinished, for it rained all next day from 10am till 10am next day, when I left for London.

I went into the T.F. to draw the next morning and began before it rained. J. had told me I might go into the Hatching House if it rained so I did and he came in also and fetched in my easel. I told him about Edith and Miss Baumer and he seemed thrilled. Then Charles came in to say someone had come to see him and he said 'I will come at once' and he went off.

I waited a little while, but it continued to rain, so I did not like to stay longer. I left the easel in the H. H. [hatching house]. On my way to the gate I came across J. talking to a gentleman. He said to me 'I don't think the rain will continue very long.' But it did and I was puzzled to know what to do, as I did not want to leave without saying goodbye and referring to our meeting again. I felt he knew so very little about me! So from my bedroom window, which faced the Mill, I watched about the time he usually came in the afternoon and as soon as I saw him coming I went down and went into the T. F. in mac and umbrella and little dark-blue hat and we had another little chat in our little H. H. We discussed getting a car and he said he objected to getting his hands oily. He said he did not mind honest dirt – mud and water, and I pointed out that my doctor brother chauffeured his own car and managed to keep his hands nice. 'Does he?' said J. 'Yes,' I said, 'he has to'. 'It's very clever of him' said J. (At the beginning he asked me to sit down and I said 'Can you spare the time?' He looked at his watch and said he could spare 5 minutes. So I sat down.) We also discovered that both our eldest brothers had been in India and in the army.

I, 'You said that you might come and see me in the Lake District.'

He, 'I should like to – <u>very much</u>' (low and intense)

He, 'Would it be any use if I sent my sister[11] to call on you? She is rather an invalid, not very strong – rather a poor thing. She insists on living there all by herself, though we none of us want her to (and his eyes were hard, the only time I have seen them so). She does not care about paintings, but is fond of music.' Of course I said I should be very pleased if she would call. I also told him there was some ointment my brother and his family in York used to protect their hands from dirt, when he told me someone had said they could get him a motor for £10, but I could not remember the name.

We also discussed cycling and that it was not wise to do too much. He had cycled to a place on business 17 miles each way and admitted it was rather much. He also said, 'I am very light.' He seemed afraid of feeling faint cycling, if he missed his tea! I said it must be time to go, as the little fish must not go hungry. He looked at his watch and said it was just time. He took my easel and said 'I will take it to the gate for you.' I wondered a little, why not to the Hotel! So we parted at the gate in pouring rain and he said in a feeling voice 'I am very sorry you are going.'

It rained on till 10am next morning and I left by the bus for Cirencester and did not see him again. So ended 4 most memorable days.

So I returned to the Club, my feeling for J. not gone, but very much stronger and also with the impression that he was not indifferent.

I longed to communicate with him in some way and having remembered the name of the ointment for the hands I had mentioned in our parting interview I decided to write and tell him what it was.

I first made sure of the correct name 'Peldo' [or 'Peldow'] by asking the chemist at the corner. I wrote a quite short but friendly little letter and felt great pleasure at the thought that he would be sure to answer it. To make sure (as I thought) I gave my address in Paris.

In Paris I found it very difficult to settle down to work or take a proper interest in it.

The important question seemed to be, not, can I do portraits? but 'does he care?' I was pleased to find I was near Notre Dame, but when I got inside I found myself not so much looking at the building, as taking advantage of the seclusion to sit down and consider carefully the pros and cons of the important question. On the whole the yeas had it and my hopes seemed justified. Then came the question, was I to go straight home and hope he might some time come. I remember I had asked him if he did not miss the mountains and he said no and that he disliked the loneliness of Brantwood and he liked to be able to go and have dinner with a friend any evening when he had tired of his own company. Also that he once said 'I ought to be there with my brother and sister, but it is difficult for me to get away.' So I felt it would be well to make sure of our meeting again, as we seemed mutually attracted and had only ourselves to please. I had originally intended spending 2 months in Paris, but I had lost one week by going back to B. [Bibury] and

I felt that, compared with a life happiness, or even the chance of it, the extra time in Paris was as nothing. So after much considering (and once I was sitting in the Champs Elysees gardens and thinking deeply about it when I was only roused by 2 ladies raising their voices to ask me a question as I had taken no notice at first) I decided to stay one month in Paris and then return to Bibury staying only 2 nights in London.

All this time the expected letter never came. Each day I looked hopefully at the rack but in vain. I simply could not believe that J. could do anything not quite polite and I thought he must have lost my letter with the address, or sent a letter which had not arrived.

After waiting a fortnight I decided to take the bull by the horns and find out from J. himself whether he had answered. So I wrote to him to tell him I thought a little B. would do me good after the nerve-wracking streets of Paris and asked him if he knew of any rooms with an Aladdin Lamp. And towards the end I 'wonder whether you got my letter about the Peldow?'

The answer this time came by return and was a terrible blow. He had never written and admitted that he ought to have. I threw myself on my bed in utter misery. J. had been rude – and to me! Why, my own brothers would have replied to a lady's letter even if they had not cared about her. It was (and it still is even now) quite incomprehensible. Of course I had expected that he would be delighted to have a reason for writing to me.

I almost wrote at once to say I had changed my plans and was not coming to B. but decided to do nothing hastily, as I felt so strongly about it. The letter came I think on Friday – I waited till Sunday. That morning I went to the Louvre – church being quite impossible. After much debating I felt that I must forgive him, or what was love worth. Then I felt a great calm and wrote a kind letter, admitting that I had perhaps expected an answer, but that the fault being confessed, it received full absolution. And to cheer him I praised his finding rooms with the Aladdin lamp and thanked him for going himself.

So on October 20th I returned to B. – my 3rd visit. The next morning I met J. on his chestnut. He always goes for a gentle ride before going into the farm. Of course I had pictured our first meeting, after a whole month, as very thrilling and delightful. He said, in an unmoved voice, 'I am very glad to see you back again.' Hurt by his coolness, I said 'I beg your pardon'. And he repeated it. I managed with an effort to say something about painting autumn tints and that they had been beautiful as I came in the train. He said 'Yes, they are later here'. And started his horse going again and patting it on the back. I felt half stunned with the pain and disappointment and did not go inside the farm that morning, indeed felt that I did not want to go in at all, if that was all he cared. I sat on the wall outside and tried to divert my mind by drawing in a sketch. However, in the afternoon I decided it was a pity not to give us the chance I had come for and went in. He came up with Charles and spoke and asked 'How did you like Paris?' I said 'Very much. You must come to tea on Sunday and hear all about it'. And he smiled and looked meaningly [sic] at my hat (which was one I had bought in Paris, with a pretty lighter blue bow on the dark blue felt). I answered the expressive smile with one which acknowledged his unspoken meaning, i.e. that the hat came from Paris. That smile cleared away my bruised feeling and made me happy again, but it was the only real smile he gave me during all that visit. Why, I don't know. He also agreed to come to tea on Sunday.

I think it rained on Saturday, and that we did not meet again until Sunday tea time. I was ready for him at 4.30 but he did not come till 5. I was sorry, as I wanted to show him my sketches of B, which I had brought back chiefly to show him and also the Evening Service began at 6, it left us little time. I remarked as he came in, 'You haven't left us much time' and asked if I might show him my sketches. The light was fading, so I put him in a chair near the window and showed him first the one of the mill door and stream and little bridge. He looked at it carefully and said 'That is very good, what beautiful colour; I didn't know you had done anything as good as that!' And then, just as Mrs C. came in with the tea, 'I am probably saying quite the wrong thing!' Of course I was delighted. I showed him the others, including one of the mill with him in it and told him it was meant for him. He praised all, but asked to see the first one again. Of the 'Willery with duck pond', he said 'It is very good, but not the subject that this is'. Then we had tea. He takes his without milk or sugar. I asked if it was as he liked it and he said 'It is just perfect'. I asked him had he been to Paris and he said once, a long time ago, with his father. He had not cared much for it and thought all the Boulevards were so alike! I had thought that we should have walked together to the Church, but he said he must go back to the Hatching House to do something with the water, so he left before six. He said, "I want you to come to tea with me' but looked worried. And I went to church alone and sat two or three seats behind him. He did not join me coming out, as I had also hoped! So I went back alone and it was so pitch dark that I had difficulty in finding the house and went beyond it.

The next 3 or 4 mornings I painted the Mill with the trees in their autumn tints, from a spot not far from the H. H. It was rainy and very wet underfoot and J. offered me a board to put my feet on and sent Charles with it. Charles lingered, watching me paint and J. had to stand a moment waiting for him. I also painted in the farm in the afternoons. It was nice to feel free from children and also I wanted us to meet as often as possible! Every morning and afternoon, unless he was away, J. came to see my work and exchange a few words, but he never asked me to tea or proposed doing anything with me or asked me to come round the farm with him. I was not happy about that Mill picture (and indeed no-one has really liked it since) but J. came by and said, in a feeling voice, 'You have got beautiful colouring'. Agitated and worried I said 'Do you really think so?' in a rather tragic voice and he said he did. So I was comforted, though not convinced.

I would have liked to have asked him to tea on my birthday, 27th, but put it off till the day, hoping he might ask me. He came up rather early and said he was going to a Concert at Cheltenham. It was a horrid blow. I decided to say nothing about its being my birthday and asked how he was going. He said 'Miss – is taking me in her car, so I can go comfortably'. He said who was playing and that he preferred someone else. I said I did not know them, as I was not musical. He answered 'I should have thought you would have been'. So the rest of the day I was alone and the looked-forward-to birthday fell very flat.

When it rained, I used to take refuge with my things in the H. H. Sometimes he came too. Once we had a longish wait in the morning and both sat down and had a talk and he asked did I know anything about stained glass. I said 'No'. He seemed disappointed and told me how some rich local man had wanted to put up a stained glass window over the B. church altar. The top part was not so bad, but below was a representation of himself driving, I think, a coach. He said 'They left it to me to decide – as churchwarden one has some influence and I said I could not pass it, that it was as if I had wanted to put in a window with me wearing trout-flies in my hat! They kindly said they would wish for nothing better! Then I went to London and went with my father to see the original design. And he said, 'My son Arthur has brought me to see your window' etc. They liked the window itself very much but still disliked the lower part but finally J. sent it to the Bishop and he refused to allow it.

Then he had to go by the bus to C -, so he changed his boots and I looked out of the door, not to embarrass him. After he left I walked up and down outside the hut and on his way he turned and saw me and raised his hat with a smile and I waved my hand. It was one of the happiest moments of my life.

One day, when he was going for his usual morning ride before coming into the farm, I looked round and saw him take off his cap and wave it several times round his head, but to whom, or what for, I never discovered, and had not the courage (or impertinence!) to ask him.

Another morning when he came up as usual to speak to me, he said 'I daren't tell you what happened this morning, it was like a nightmare'. He said, when Charles passed by the Mill on his way to the blacksmith to get something done to the 'old horse', he noticed that the stream was empty – no water in it and when J. came, he found the fish standing on their heads. One of his neighbours, a Colonel Markham (or some such name), had turned the water off entirely. I asked why? He said 'You may well ask why!' It seems the Col. had had workmen doing some digging out on his land and turned the water off with selfish disregard for J. He said 'You could have walked across in your galoshes' and glanced down at my brown galoshes. J. went off forthwith on his bicycle and interviewed the selfish Col. and told me that he had told him he must have something drawn up by his lawyer so that it could not happen again. He said it was not the first time it had happened.

Another morning he told me 'We were up until 11 last night clearing away fallen leaves'. It had been a windy night. I said 'Would they do harm?' and he said they would prevent the water from running properly. He said 'The moon came out and it was beautiful at one o'clock'. I answered 'I am afraid I was asleep then', and I saw him smile, as he moved away.

Another morning he told me his brother had written and told him that a picture of a Doge, by Titian, which his people had sold for £6,000, had been resold for £22,000 and he added 'It is a lot of money'. I said it was a shame, but he did not seem bitter about it, quite gentle.

When it came to within 4 days of my leaving, I felt I must make an effort as he showed no sign. So on Friday evening I again asked him to tea, this time on Monday, as Sunday left so little time. And I told him I was leaving on the Wednesday. He looked sad and said in a feeling voice 'I am sorry you are going, I hoped you would have stayed all the autumn to paint the tints'. I said I was going to a friend who had rheumatoid arthritis. Then he said 'Are you sure I shan't bore you?' I couldn't help laughing at the idea, though I felt it was rather rude and stupid of me. But the idea of his boring me when two separate times I had been obliged to return just to see more of him!! I just said 'No, you won't bore me!' And he replied 'Then I shall be very pleased to come'.

On Saturday evening I had finished my sketch when he came and I put down my brushes and followed him and asked if I might see the fish. So he showed me some troutlets about 5 inches long which he said were 1 year old. He said 'They probably look small to you; they look quite big to me'. Then he moved on and seemed (to my surprise) unwilling for me to come with him and said 'There is nothing more to see here'. And when I still came, he said 'I wanted to do some sweeping before it gets dark'. But he talked about the dusky weed that grew up in the water. So I went back, feeling rather rebuffed and sore.

On Sunday morning I went to Church and he read the lessons as usual and came out laughing and talking with his friends the L-Ds and took no notice of me.

In the evening it was raining, but as it was our last Sunday evening I went to Church again, in my mac, and he came in later in his. I sat about three seats behind as usual, but on the opposite side. After the Service, he made rather a dash for his mac, which was in the pew in front of him, and rather hurried out. Bye-the-bye, his side of the aisle was almost empty that evening and he sat quite by himself in his pew. I got out before him, but he made a short cut by going along an empty pew and as he passed I smiled at him, but he did not respond. Why, I don't know. So I got out first into the darkness and I wondered if it was me he was hurrying up to go with, when I heard a woman's voice behind and his voice answered very pleasantly. So I thought, no, it is not me, and went on quickly, feeling hurt. But in another moment he was beside me and opening with his usual sympathetic remark that he was afraid the weather was not good for my work. Though it was not actually raining then. I said it had been a fine sunset when I was walking along the road to Fairford or rather back. And he said 'What my sister[12] and I called a David Farquerson[13] effect. We were very fond of his pictures. But perhaps you like them too?' I said 'Yes, I do'. And after we had discussed Farquerson a bit, I said, 'You looked quite lonely in your pew tonight'. He answered, 'Yes, people will always sit in the same pew, I don't know why. I allow the L-Ds to sit in mine'.

As it was so dark, I kept bumping up against him. For myself I did not mind and would have liked to have asked to take his arm! but was afraid he might think me forward! so refrained and walked a little further away. As we got near my lodgings I said, 'I am somewhere here. Last Sunday it was so dark I walked beyond', rather hoping he might take it as a hint that he might have seen me home! He only said 'Did you?' And that I must remember the step. And about the tea next day he said he wanted to ask me but would rather come to me, as he might not get up (the village) in time and hoped I did not mind; I rather stupidly said 'It will be a great pleasure'. So we parted with a short 'Good-bye'. I felt very pleased and happy.

On Monday he came to tea. I had hurried over my afternoon sketch of autumn tints and water and sunset in the farm, in order to get ready before he came, but he did not come till five. He came in looking anxious and said 'I am afraid I am late'. But I replied, 'No, it has only just struck five'. So he looked relieved and said 'Then that is all right'. And looking round, caught sight of my sketches put up in a row above the sofa, and said 'Don't they look nice!' And went over to see them. About my last morning one he said 'I was looking at it at lunch time. I took the liberty of moving it'. I asked which he liked best and he said of the Old Mill in autumn tints, 'Of course that is perfect'. He knelt down to see them better. But I think he liked the one of the large, smooth pond the best, then tea came and he said he preferred to sit 'on the other side', i.e. away from the fire, which pleased me, not coddly [i.e. molly-coddled]. I asked if his tea was right – remembering that he took neither sugar nor milk – and he answered 'Just perfect'. I said I would let him taste the buns first to see if they were cocoanut and he said they were. But afterwards I found they were not! Then I asked him to sit in the gentleman's chair, so he told me about the travelling van of whom he bought 2 curry brushes, and they left 2 chairs at the house, and his sister took them in, not knowing, and they called them 'the Gentleman's Chair' and 'the Lady's Chair'. And his comment was 'Really, people like that deserve to get on!' Then he told me about Dr Parsons and his father and the Dr saying 'I told him to go to the Devil' and collapsing in tears and had to be revived with port. I asked about his garden in his home in B. where he had lived with his sister and he said it was not large but everything was good. We spoke of Ruskin's books and he offered to lend me some, but as I was leaving in 2 days, it seemed rather futile! I found he did not play Bridge or chess, though Ruskin played the latter. He was playing the piano and played with the architect who lived in the same house. I thought he seemed quite a 'limpet' and satisfied with his life and pursuits and surroundings. I asked if he had been in Paris and he said, 'Once, a long time ago' when there was an Exhibition on and he and his sister went about in it in bath chairs. He did not care for Paris, found the Boulevards all alike. I was disappointed, as I had found it interesting and amusing and had wished he had been with me to enjoy it.

He got up to go at 7. I said 'Don't hurry away'. But he said he had some writing to do. And then he told me about the young couple in the car, who wanted to buy a fish and he asked 'Is it to keep?' and they said 'No'. He – 'Is it to eat?' Again, 'No.' He 'Then if it is not a rude question, what is it for?' They – To give to a friend for a wedding present, stuffed! He said it was difficult to stuff them well and would it not be better to have a picture made of one and give that and he knew an artist who could do it for them (me). So they were to think it over and he might get me a fish to paint any time. However, it never came!

Just as he was leaving, I said lightly 'How do you like my dog?' referring to a charcoal sketch of the head of the dog belonging to my landlady – Mrs C. He glanced at it and said 'Is it charcoal?' I said 'yes' and he went. (But two days ago, nearly 8½ months later, he writes 'The dog you did for Mrs C. is wonderful', so I gather that he has seen it since; probably visiting other lady artists!) I felt strangely unmoved that evening, why I don't know.

Next morning, my last day, there was a Meet at the S- Hotel [the Swan Hotel], close by. My landlady and her daughter went and I went a little later and stood on the pavement. There were quite a lot of hunters, both sexes. Presently I saw J. on his old chestnut, with its white forehead, coming slowly down and rather, as I flattered myself, looking about for someone. He stopped and spoke to a smartish lady about a concert. And then saw me and moved his horse close. He said he was afraid the hunt was hindering my painting, but it would not be long. I asked, should I see him to say good bye? He said 'Tomorrow'. And I said 'I shan't be there tomorrow, as I am going'. So he said he would not be away long and would come to the farm in the afternoon, and moved to one side and presently the whole hunt moved off. I felt disinclined to paint so took a walk and I saw him again, as the hunters turned back and went along the very road I wanted to explore, but I held back and he didn't see me.

I had intended to sketch in the afternoon, but it rained. I had to fetch my easel from the H. House and hoped to be able to time my going for it so as to meet John. I saw the hunting folk returning by ones and twos soon after lunch, so thought by going about 4 to give him time for lunch and to get down. But when I got to the H. H., as usual in mackintosh and umbrella, it was empty. I was much puzzled to know what to do. To wait for him seemed hardly the thing and yet to leave without saying goodbye was impossible! Then I thought I could fasten a strip of paper to the chair, suggesting that he should come and see me in the evening. Just as I was going to do it, I looked up and saw him coming in the distance from the Mill entrance, and still dressed in his dark hunting clothes. I saw a wave of emotion pass over his face when he caught sight of me. I was very stupid that afternoon and only said something about his having come just in time and had not the sense to say that I had come to fetch my easel, so that it looked (and I felt then that it did) as if I were just looking out for him!

He asked, had I got wet. I said, no, had he. He said 'No, not really, any how it doesn't matter for us!'

I – 'Why not?'

He – 'Oh – it is all in the day's work'.

I – 'It was nice to see the hunt – it made me feel *I* wanted to be on a horse again'.

He – 'Yes, it is a pretty sight'.

I – 'I think the riding is splendid, but I don't like the actual hunting'.

(Before that he told me they had soon found a fox and I asked did they kill it and he said 'Yes – I was sorry, as it showed great pluck and skill'. I was very pleased he said he was sorry.)

He – 'No – Stupid hunting people, as my father says'.

I – 'Does he disapprove?'

He – 'Yes – he does in a way and yet he has spoken of my sister and me to other people as if he were proud of our hunting.'

Also he said: 'Really in this county, the fox gets away 5 times out of six and they have to be killed on account of their killing the chickens and ducks. He said he went round and paid compensation to the owners when the foxes killed their fowls or ducks and he thought they were well paid for them'.

I had felt it was quite time for me to go, but he spoke first and said 'Well, I must go – good bye!' I said 'Good-bye' and we shook hands and he held mine in a long, firm grasp, which I returned.

Then he turned to go and I said 'Thank you so much' but he stopped me quickly with 'Not at all' and as he went out of the little house, turned and said 'I shall write to my sister – little Violet we call her – When do you go to Outgate?' I said 'Nov. 15' and he walked quickly away in the pouring rain towards the fish canals. I went back into the houselet and fetched my easel and could not help feeling how odd it must look to some people passing along the road to see him striding away and me carrying my easel and umbrella by myself to the gate.

I felt very annoyed with myself for not having said I must go before he did, as if I had outstayed my welcome! And if I wept bitter tears of mortification that night there was only One who saw it in the darkness.

Notes

Introduction

1. A. Carreras and C. Josephson, 'Aggregate growth, 1870-1914: growing at the production frontier' in S. Broadberry & K. H. O'Rourke (eds.), *The Cambridge Economic History of Modern Europe*, vol.2, 1870-Present (Cambridge 2010), p.32.
2. While this statement may strike the reader as rather contentious, the author maintains that the collapse of four empires, the world's first Communist Government, the growing enfranchisement of women and a raft of other changes does constitute the end of one civilisation (using the OED's definition as, 'the society, culture, and way of life of a particular area') and the start of another in Europe. That is not to say that these changes were not going to happen in any case, merely that they did not exist before the war and did so afterwards.
3. J. Bishop., *The Illustrated London News: Social History of the First World War* (Angus & Robertson 1982), foreword by Lord Blake, p.7.
4. Gresham College lecture given by Professor Chris Clark, (Museum of London, 29th September 2014), transcript available from the Gresham website: http://www.gresham.ac.uk/lectures-and-events/sleepwalkers-how-europe-went-to-war-in-1914.
5. There has been debate over who started the war since the 'War Guilt Clause' in the Treaty of Versailles in 1919 which placed the blame firmly on Germany. This was widely challenged and rejected in Germany and by some intellectuals in other nations. Fritz Fischer's *Germany's Aims in the First World War* ignited the debate again by placing the blame with German elites. The sheer volume of books that touch on the origins of the war and Germany's role in its creation is immense. A few worthwhile places to start are: Christopher Clark's *The Sleepwalkers;* Sean McMeekin's *The Russian Origins of the First World War;* A.J.P. Taylor's *War by Time-Table: How the First World War Began;* and Margaret Macmillan's *The War that Ended Peace.*
6. D. Reynolds., *The Long Shadow: The Great War and the Twentieth Century* (Simon & Schuster 2013), p.XVIII.

Chapter 1

1. The use of 'tremendous' is noteworthy, as it has multiple meanings and thus Mabel could be conveying fearfulness, scale, excitement or awe.

Chapter 2
1. *The Times*, 3 July, 1916.
2. J. Horne., 'Atrocities and war crimes' in J. Winter (ed), *The Cambridge History of The First World War* Vol, 1, Cambridge 2014, p.569.

Chapter 4
1. From Harold Macmillan's foreword in J. S. Goodall, *An Edwardian Summer*, Macmillan 1976, p.1.
2. While in 1916 a new maid is taken on, from this point until the end of the war it seems that Mabel only had two maids.
3. *The Sinking of the Lusitania* by Winsor McCay, 1918.
4. Burnham, K. *York In The Great War*, Pen & Sword 2014, p. 43.
5. *Ibid*, p.47.
6. Reciting prayers while holding rosary beads, a practice usually taken to indicate Catholic faith.
7. 1117 deaths and around 3,000 injuries from both Zeppelin and plane attacks. See J. Bishop, *The Illustrated London News: Social History of the First World War*, Angus & Robertson 1982, p.77.
8. Cervantes said this in his novel *Don Quixote*, first published in 1605. A copy of this was released by Project Gutenberg in 2004. The quote in this translation can be found on page 581 and reads as 'with bread all sorrows are less', the text is available at http://publicliterature.org/pdf/996.pdf.
9. Kramer, A., Blockade and economic warfare, in Winter, J. (ed.), *The Cambridge History of the First World War*, Vol. II, p.40.
10. *Ibid*, p.461.

Chapter 6
1. Meaning civilian dress.

Chapter 7
1. Saturday 1 August 1914. By this time Austria has declared war on Serbia and Germany has declared war on Russia.
2. This space was left blank in the diary for Mabel to insert the names of the countries later. At this point she may be unclear exactly which countries have now declared war.
3. I.e. civilian dress.
4. Valise in this sense does not mean a suitcase but a portable bed-roll.
5. Strensall Camp is a military camp about six miles north of York, now known as Queen Elizabeth II Barracks.
6. Now called Aachen, on the border between Belgium and Germany, short for Aix La Chapelle.
7. Given his time at Heidelberg.

8. The battle of Gumbinnen (started 20 August 1914).
9. She may mean Tsingtao.
10. The Siege of Namur (20–25 August 1914).
11. Meuse or Maas is a river running through France and Belgium, with the Belgian town Dinant on its bank.
12. The Battle of Lorraine took place around this time and French forces initially retreated on the 25th of August.
13. Fyling Hall, Fylingdales, on the coast between Whitby and Scarborough, is a Grade II listed building (now a school), built by John Barry in 1819.
14. The elder Miss Barry married into the Dunnington-Jefferson family of Thorganby Hall, to the south-west of York.
15. Part of the Battle of Galicia (23 August to 11 September 1914).
16. Archangel, or Arkhangelsk, is a seaport in Northern Russia.
17. It is said that the Germans could see the Eiffel Tower and that this battle was vital to the defence of Paris.
18. Edward Wood was the MP for Ripon and was later Lord Irwin, Viceroy of India, and then 3rd Viscount Lord Halifax. (He was in fact 6 ft 5 ins inches tall, not seven foot as Henry asserts.)
19. A small settlement in rural British Columbia.
20. A type of battleship with one or two large guns and a shallow draft.
21. SMS *Karlsruhe*.
22. Dr Charles Sarolea, war correspondent for the *Daily Chronicle* and author of *How Belgium Saved Europe* (1915). He was a noted academic, giving lecture tours in the United States and Canada in 1915.
23. Most probably HMS *Halcyon*.
24. Franz Joseph, Prince of Hohenzollern-Emden.
25. Field Marshall Roderick Sleigh Roberts, 1st Earl Roberts, Lord Roberts of Kandahar, was a hugely popular and successful general. Kipling wrote a poem to commemorate his death.
26. RMS *Missanabie*.
27. This is four months after the war started.
28. 30hp Daimler bought by Henry in 1904.
29. Battle of the Falkland Islands (8 December 1914).
30. Mrs Jencken and her husband, Colonel Jencken, were friends of Mabel's. Col. Francis John Jencken became Surgeon-General, Army Medical Services.
31. Waltz.
32. A small village about four miles from York.
33. Battle of Ardahan (25 December 1914 – 18 January 1915).
34. All these figures are in shillings.
35. This cannot be right as there was no *Karlsruhe* at this time. It had been sunk on 4 November 1914, indicating the degree of accuracy Mabel got from the papers.

36. Wilfred was serving as a 2nd Lt. 3rd Royal Fusiliers (City of London Regiment) and was stationed at Gravenstafel Ridge, Ypres. Poison gas was used for the first time by the Germans on 22nd April and it is possible Wilfred was killed by the gas. He was originally reported as killed in action sometime between 22 and 29 April, and only later confirmed that he died on 25 April. After leaving school he won a History Scholarship to Christ Church, Oxford, graduating in 1910. He was studying law at the Middle Temple at the outbreak of the War. No known grave.
37. Replaced by South Africa House in 1935.
38. Skelton Grange farmhouse, outside York, still exists.
39. A family friend, later Mabel's nephew's Godmother, who was for a time supposedly in love with Henry.
40. Mabel appears to mean Erich von Falkenhayn, German Chief of Staff 1914–16.
41. General Sir Henry Macleod Leslie Rundle.
42. Meaning static air, no wind.
43. A one-piece hood with mica eyepiece, the Hypo helmet or British Smoke Hood was designed to protect against chlorine gas for up to three hours. It came into use in June 1915.
44. The Essex Regiment 1st Garrison Battalion was formed on 21 July 1915 from officers and men unfit for direct combat due to age or infirmity, to undertake police and guard duties. With Stuart were 26 other officers and 984 other ranks. According to Regimental records, on 24 August they embarked for Gallipoli from Devonport via Mudros, arriving 3 September and leaving for Egypt in February 1916. However, Stuart seems to have been stationed at Lemnos, not Gallipoli, before going to Egypt.
45. Actually Lieutenant-Colonel John Cassells Monteith, killed in action 1 October 1915 aged 39. He was second in command of 2nd Battalion, Bedford Regiment. He lived at Moniaive, Dumfriesshire.
46. The home of Evans' mother in Wales.
47. This was the last voluntary scheme before conscription.
48. Mabel's first cousin once removed.
49. In February 1916 the Battalion was transferred to Mex Camp, Egypt and from there to Ismailia (Ishmalia) where part of the Battalion was sent to Ballah and Shallufa for patrol and guard work.
50. In April 1916 the Battalion was sent to Zagazig, the main supply depot in Egypt, some forty miles from Cairo.
51. Aislaby is a small village about three miles from Whitby in North Yorkshire. It is not clear what the 'S.O.' refers to.
52. I.e. reciting prayers while holding rosary beads.
53. Read scullery.
54. Hemingford Grey is a village close to St Ives in Cambridgeshire.

Epilogue
1. Henry lived to see his sons follow his footsteps when they served during the Second World War and were involved in the Normandy Landings of 1944.
2. Rising approximately from 3.2 to 4.1 million. See Thom, D., 'Women and work in wartime Britain', in Wall, R. & Winter, J. (eds.), *The Upheaval of War: Family Work and Welfare in Europe, 1914–18*, Cambridge 1988, p.307.
3. See Art.IWM PST 11675 in the Imperial War Museum Collection for a copy.
4. She references meat eating in the diary but was known as a vegetarian by the mid-1920s.

Appendix
1. Referencing the Second Boer War (1899–1902).
2. Louis Botha, prominent figure for the Boers against the British during the Boer War but led troops against German South West Africa and put down a Boer rebellion during the First World War.
3. Probably meaning Kaiser Wilhelm the II, the German Emperor.
4. An eighteenth century term, using a literary term for Britain and accusing the British of treachery.
5. Secretary of State for the Imperial German Navy, 1897–1916.
6. Meaning 'the day', i.e. the day German supremacy begins.
7. The country home of William Morris from 1871 until his death in 1896.
8. Famously and picturesque 17th century weavers' cottages, in Bibury.
9. A well-known poet, 1858–1935.
10. Ruskin was ill for the last eleven years of his life, and hardly spoke.
11. Violet Severn, 1880–1940.
12. Lily Severn, who lived at Bibury and died in 1920.
13. David Farquharson, painter, 1839–1907.

Bibliography

Historical Works

Adie, K., *Fighting on the Home Front: The Legacy of Women in World War One*, Hodder 2013

Bilbrough, M.E., *My War Diary 1914–1918*, Ebury Press 2014

Bishop, J., *The Illustrated London News: Social History of the First World War*, Angus & Robertson 1982

Broadberry, S. & O'Rourke, H.K. (eds.), *The Cambridge Economic History of Modern Europe: Volume 2, 1870 to the Present*, Cambridge 2010

Burnham, K., *York In The Great War*, Pen & Sword Books 2014

Charman, T., *The First World War on the Home Front*, Andre Deutsch 2014

Chris, C., *The Sleepwalkers: How Europe Went to War in 1914*, Allen Lane 2012

Ferguson, N., *The Pity of War: Explaining World War One*, Penguin 1998

Gilbert, M., *First World War Atlas*, Weidenfeld and Nicolson, 1970

Graves, R., *Goodbye To All That*, (Jonathan Cape 1929) Penguin 2000

Mallinson, A., *1914 Fight the Good Fight: Britain, the Army & the Coming of the First World War*, Bantam Press 2013

Marwick, A., *The Deluge*, Bodley Head 1965

Newman, V., *We Also Served: The Forgotten Women of the First World War*, Pen & Sword 2014

Philpott, W., *Bloody Victory: The Sacrifice on the Somme*, Abacus 2009

Reynolds, D., *The Long Shadow: The Great War and the Twentieth Century*, Simon & Schuster 2013

Richards, I., Goodson, B. J., Morris, A. J., *A Sketch-Map History of the Great War and After 1914–1915*, George G. Harrap & Co. Ltd, 1938

Roynon, G., *Home Fires Burning: The Great War Diaries of Georgina Lee*, The History Press 2009

Scales, L. (Scales, P. ed.), *A Home Front Diary 1914–1918*, Amberley 2014

Stone, N., *A Short WWI History*, Penguin 2007

Strachan, H., *The First World War*, Simon & Schuster (first pub. 2003) 2014

Taylor, P.J.A., *The First World War: An Illustrated History*, (Hamilton 1963) Penguin 1966

Tootze, A., *The Deluge: The Great War and the Remaking of Global Order*, Penguin 2015

Tuchman, W.B., *The Guns of August*, Macmillan 1962

Wall, R. & Winter, J. (eds.), *The Upheaval of War: Family Work and Welfare in Europe, 1914–18*, Cambridge 1988

Winter, J., *The Cambridge History of the First World War*, vols. 1–3, Cambridge 2014

Fictional Works

Barrie, M.J., *Admirable Crichton* (play published 1902), The Echo Library 2007

Cervantes, M., *Don Quixote*, (first pub. 1605), Project Gutenberg version available at http://publicliterature.org/pdf/996.pdf 2004

Ford, M.F., *Parade's End*, Wordsworth 2013

Goodall, S.J., *An Edwardian Summer*, Macmillan 1976

Hemingway, E., *A Farewell to Arms*, (Scribner 1929) Random House 2012

Remarque, M.E., *All Quiet on the Western Front*, (Ullstein 1929) Random House 2005

Sassoon, S., *Memoirs of a Fox-hunting Man*, (Faber and Faber 1928) Penguin 2013

Wells, G.H., *Kipps: The Story of A Simple Soul*, Macmillan 1905

Wells, G.H., *Mr. Britling Sees It Through*, (first pub. 1916) Waterlow & Sons 1933

Photo Acknowledgments

Figures: 1–3, 6, 13–23, 26–28, 30–35, 37–42, 44–9 are from the Goode family collection which holds copyright for them.

The Author is immensely grateful for the following photos, given with kind permission by:

Royal Pavilion and Museums, Brighton & Hove for figures: 7–9, 24, 29, 36 & 43

Tony Allen, whose wonderful collection of First World War postcards and research is available at www.worldwar1postcards.com, for figures: 4–5, 10–12 & 25

The cover of this book also includes two postcards from Tony Allen's collection (both at the top of the back cover).

All other images used in the cover are from the Goode family collection which holds copyright for them.

Index

Locators for pictures and figures are denoted in *italics*.